DUCATI

DUCATI

SuperBikes

851, 888, 916

PAOLO CONTI

DUCATI

SuperBikes

851, 888, 916

Motorbooks International
Publishers & Wholesalers ®

Acknowledgements
The author and the publisher would like to thank for their help the engineers Massimo Bordi, general manager of Ducati, and Claudio Domenicali, Ducati racing director, who gave freely of their scant free time to correct the text. Special thanks also go to Nadia Pavignani and Eliana Chieruzzi of the Ducati press office, for their help in solving problems of all sorts. The translator would like to thank Christopher McNellis for his generous assistance and advice on technical terminology.

Translation
Antony Shugaar

This edition first published in 1995 by Motorbooks International Publishers & Wholesalers,
PO Box 2 , 729 Prospect Avenue,PO Box 1, Osceola, WI 54020 USA
© 1995 Giorgio Nada Editore, Vimodrone (Milan).

Library of Congress Cataloging-in Publication Data Available.
ISBN 0 - 7603 - 0222 - 7

Printed and bound in Italy.

CONTENTS

INTRODUCTION

The name of the most phenomenal motorcycle of the nineties is Ducati "Desmoquattro." The name is a succinct way of describing the main distinguishing technical feature of the Ducati 748, 851, 888, and 916—behind that name is a series of motorcycles that have brought a major Italian motorcycle manufacture into the spotlight—or perhaps we should say, *back* into the spotlight—both in commercial and

racing terms. After the glory of its past history, with the spectacular performance of its small- and medium-displacement single-cylinder bikes and its bevel-drive and belt-drive L-2 bikes (750 and 900), Ducati has returned to major standing among motorcycle manufacturers.

It will be the various versions of the 851, 888, and 916 that will take Ducati back over the paths of glory blazed in

On the preceding page, the 916 Superbike, presented in 1994 and destined to carry on the tradition of the entire Desmoquattro series, combined impressive technical qualities with refined styling. Left, Desmoquattro means, above all, racing: in this photograph, Raymond Roche rides his 851 during the 1989 season. The French racer claims the distinction of having been the first to ride the Bolognese motorcycle to a world Superbike championship, and to have taken part in the development and evolution that made Ducati the true unrivaled leader in the category. Below, the 851 Superbike Strada, first of the Desmoquattro series to be sold for normal street use.

This motorcycle was officially presented in 1988, immediately following the Superbike Kit model, which was intended for racing. The two motorcycles are quite similar, in technical terms. Both stand out from all later versions of the Desmoquattro series in their tricolor paint, as if they were trying to underscore the Italian provenance of Ducati technology.

the fifties by its Gran Sport 100 and 125, often known as the Marianna.

These paths of glory continued with the Desmo 250-350-450 racing bikes, and then with the models powered by twin-cylinder engines, with desmodromic valve gear, since 1973 the very emblem of Ducati motorcycles.

Right up to the dawn of the eighties, the name Ducati was synonymous with spectacular victories and solid tradition in the field of road racing—qualities that only added to the luster of the name of the Bolognese manufacturer.

Great as that reputation was, however, the mass-produced bikes fell somewhat short. As the years went by, this glaring contrast worsened, sadly undermining the image of Ducati. The commercial repercussions were nasty, and levels of production sagged and dwindled, to as low as a thousand bikes a year.

The turning point came in 1985, when Ducati became part

With the Desmoquattro series, Ducati had hardly "forgotten" the great racing tradition it had acquired in endurance racing. Thus, the debut of the motorcycles that marked such a great technical turning point for Ducati as a manufacturer took place at that great classic of endurance races, the 24-hour race of Le Mans. Ducati's official participation continued through the years that followed, as you can see from the photograph shown here of the 916 that ran in the 1995 edition of the Bol d'Or, entered by the French Ducati importer.

On the following page, on the other hand, you will see a more customary photograph of the racing anatomy of the Desmoquattro series, with Baldassare Monti (17) riding the 888 Corsa during a race of the 1993 Superbike world championship. The Parma-born racer, who in this photograph has just passed a rival, rode Ducati to win an Italian national championship. In his race for the world title, he saw his dreams shattered by a bad spill that also spelled the end of his racing career.

of the larger Cagiva Group. The ensuing change was a deep-seated one, resulting in the phenomenal development of the "Desmoquattro" and the resulting rehabilitation of the Ducati name. Let us hear these events in the words of the engineer who was responsible for them, Massimo Bordi.

"Ducati had a glorious tradition and had played a major part in the history of biking. No one can deny that. The fame that Ducati had garnered over the years from its racing division—from the fifties to the seventies—was too great a heritage to be left untapped. Indeed, that tradition was one of the foundations upon which the 'Desmoquattro' project was initially based. We could not continue to follow the same patterns as in the past: winning big on the race track without exploiting those victories in the showroom, in terms of production models.

"And when Ducati became part of the Cagiva Group, the first effort in restoring the company to its former health focused on two objectives: to rejuvenate Ducati's racing image, and to offer a reliable production bike, upon which the company could build a solid commercial structure. And both of those aspects had to meet in a single motorcycle."

With these words, Engineer Massimo Bordi begins the story of the extremely successful Ducati Desmoquattro series, regardless of the moniker employed, regardless of production year, engine size, or model name.

And his words are important ones, words which help the reader to understand the background and the subsoil in which this chapter of motorcycle history sinks its roots and to grasp the concepts that drove this remarkable undertaking, certainly the most successful manufacturing and sales campaign in the history of late-20th-century motorcycles.

The various versions—748, 851, 888, 916—are more than just models of Ducati bikes: their names summarize a bit of motorcycle history. A history of manufacturing, racing,

pop culture, and technical development. Indeed, it was by following the tradition that for so many years had made Ducati a major name on the racetracks of the world, that "Desmoquattro" came to mean racing victory, daring competition at white-hot levels, as shown by the record of 4 titles in seven championships in World Superbike, and the overwhelming superiority in the first part of the 1995 season, with eight victories in eight races. That certainly helped to reinforce the image of racing superiority. That, however, is not all. "Desmoquattro" has also come to mean exceedingly successful and popular road bikes that have made Ducati once again a name to conjure with among bike aficionados. "Desmoquattro" is above all the new direction of Casa Ducati, the motorcycles that have successfully merged tradition and technical progress, the bikes that have been racing victors and drop-dead elegant pieces of Italian style.

DESMOQUATTRO, THE LEGEND LIVES ON

In order to understand the conception and birth of the "Desmoquattro" series, let us return to the words of the mastermind behind this chapter in motorcycle history, Engineer Massimo Bordi.

"In 1985, Ducati was looking at a commercial situation in which it was struggling to keep pace with the competition. Incorporation in the Cagiva Group offered a number of new ideas. Japanese manufacturers had been building excellent

engines for a number of years—excellent both in terms of performance and reliability. And these engines had outshone the engines that we were building.

"At that time, Ducati had two engines, the 'little' Pantah, with displacement ranging from 500 to 750 cc., and the 'large' bevel-drive twins, ranging from 900 to 1000 cc. The smaller engine, admittedly with the necessary updates, is still in production in the mid-Nineties, while the bigger one

was starting to look old-fashioned in terms of design. Now those bevel-drive engines really had some astounding performance, and all one need do is look through the list of winners over the years, but they were still outmoded for use in the new bikes. Their illustrious reputations just didn't make up for their high production costs and noisy mechanical operation.

"So what Ducati needed at that point was an engine that could cover the high-power range (from 900 to 1000 cc), allowing Ducati to be competitive once again in the races for motorcycles spun off from mass production.

"So if you look at this array of motivations, you can better understand what went into Ducati's decision to design a new power plant. We needed a motorcycle that could race and win, creating great sportsmanship along the way, and at the same time, a bike that offered great performance, total reliability, and production costs that were sufficiently low to meet the competition on a level commercial playing field for production models. It was with all of these criteria in mind that we designed the new 'big' engine for Ducati bikes.

"Alongside the 'Supersport' version, however, we also needed an engine that could drive all of the possible variants of heavy motorcycles. And so we came up with what you might well call a 'modular' engine, designed for manufacture in three different versions: Economy, Gran Turismo, and Supersport. In the first of the three cases, this was an air-cooled power plant with two valves per cylinder. In short, a

On the preceding page, the "heart" of the Desmoquattro series, the engine that successfully embodied the Ducati tradition while incorporating progress and innovative engineering. Above, the 851 Superbike Kit "stripped down" in the paddock of the race track of Misano in 1988. The missing fairing reveals the latticework structure of the frame. On the right, the 1989 version of the 851 Superbike Strada.

'classic' Ducati, which greatly resembled the old Pantah. Indeed, it is quite fair to call it an updated version of the Pantah. This version was designed for use on light, reasonably priced motorcycles with low maintenance, such as the 'SS' series bikes or the 'Monster' series.

"Alongside this air-cooled power plant, we find the liquid-cooled version. This is an engine that complied with every standard around in terms of mechanical noise, perfect for use on dignified bikes, clearly for a Gran Turismo kind of motorcycle, such as the 'Paso.' Last came the 'Desmoquattro' version, which embodied the great Ducati challenge in terms of engineering and performance. The 'Desmoquattro' had been conceived as an engine capable of ensuring victories on the racetrack and high performance on the road, allowing Ducati to make that 'leap in faith' that would take the company and the name far into the future.

"And this leap into the future could not—and was not meant to be—a leap away from the history and tradition of the Ducati name, though both history and tradition would now be fully immersed in the best that motorcycle engineering could offer. The design had to incorporate a number of fundamental features, such as the twin-cylinder engine, with the 90-degree L-configuration of the cylinders, and desmodromic timing. In other words, continuity with the tradition of Ducati engines.

"A tradition that we have respected in the best of modern engineering, such as the four valves per cylinder and the liquid cooling.

"And so, the same specific features that had allowed Ducati engines of the past to become great were integrated with the finest technology available.

"Our decisions were carefully weighed, and tested by our experience in the field where technology develops best and fastest: Formula 1 racing. It is normal for someone looking for the best in terms of applied technology for power plants to turn in that direction. And we moved in that direction with an eye on the Cosworth engine.

"We made that choice because Cosworth's engine was, in my opinion, the finest one then available. Indeed, the Cosworth engine was the most advanced Formula 1 engine, as is shown by the fact that, as early as the early-Seventies, it was the first engine to make use of four-valve technology.

"In designing our engine we took our inspiration from the Cosworth thermodynamics and timing. In a certain sense, you could say that the 'Desmoquattro' was one-quarter Cosworth.

"At this point, however, perhaps I should say something more to explain the choices we made. Let us step backward

in time to 1973, when I had submitted my engineering thesis on a project that would one day become the Ducati 'Desmoquattro,' an integration of the specifications of the Bolognese power plant with the Cosworth engine.

"I am not trying to claim that I was a prophet, or in any way ahead of my time; I had simply long been a fan of Formula 1 racing, where I had particularly admired Cosworth engineering.

"I was equally fascinated by the desmodromic timing of Ducati. And so, for my thesis, I presented an air-cooled engine with four-valve desmodromic timing. Although some of the solutions were later modified and refined, such as the cooling and the shape of the manifolds [from curved to straight], in terms of practical concepts, my thesis foreshadowed what was later to become the 'Desmoquattro' engine.

"In 1986, thanks to consultation provided by Cosworth, my 1973 thesis became the foundation for the production of the prototype for the 'Desmoquattro' series.

"I do not mind admitting that Cosworth's help was crucial in three points to the success of our new engine. Their consultation helped us to develop solutions such as the narrow angle of the valves, the straight manifold intake pipes, liquid cooling, the centrally located spark plug, an appropriately designed exhaust system, and last, though certainly fundamental, electronic fuel injection.

"This type of fuel injection made it possible to keep the manifold pipes straight, thus aiding in the stoking of the chamber. In the same way, liquid cooling was inevitable if we wanted to build an advanced four-valve engine. And the same is true of the single, centrally located spark plug; when spark plugs 'proliferate,' the cylinder bore had really better be quite large.

"It may seem a bit vague to talk about an appropriately designed exhaust system, but just look at the advantages that we garner from its development year after year, and you will understand the importance of this factor.

"As the reader can probably guess, the engine of the new Ducati inherits and revitalizes the great engineering of the past, but it also keeps track of automotive engineering, which is, after all, more modern and innovative than motorcycle engineering.

"Now, I am not trying to say that motorcycles are the 'country-cousins' of automobiles. In the past twenty years,

MANY SOLUTIONS THAT WERE FIRST TESTED ON MOTORCYCLES WERE THEN ADOPTED IN AUTOMOTIVE MANUFACTURING. IT IS JUST THAT THE FOUR-STROKE ENGINE IN FORMULA 1 AUTOMOBILE RACING IS MORE ADVANCED THAN ITS MOTORCYCLE COUNTERPART.

"FORMULA 1 RACING CONSTITUTES THE PEAK OF TECHNOLOGY FOR FOUR-STROKE ENGINES—THAT'S WHY WE LOOKED THERE FIRST. ESPECIALLY IN TERMS OF PRACTICAL RESULTS.

"IN THE SEVENTIES, DUCATI HAD ALREADY BUILT A FOUR-VALVE ENGINE BUT, UNLIKE WHAT HAD HAPPENED IN FORMULA 1 RACING, WE DID NOT OBTAIN RESULTS SUFFICIENT TO MAKE US CHOOSE FOUR- OVER TWO-VALVE ENGINES. THAT WAS PROBABLY BECAUSE OF THE LACK OF INTEGRATION OF ENGINEERING KNOW-HOW THAT HAD ALREADY BEEN TESTED IN THE FIELD OF AUTOMOBILE ENGINES. THE FIRST DUCATI FOUR-VALVE ENGINE [THE GRAN PRIX 500], WHICH WAS THE ONE ON WHICH I BASED MY THESIS, HAD A VERY WIDE VALVE ANGLE AND TWO SPARK PLUGS. IN PRACTICE, IT WAS NOT A FULL-FLEDGED FOUR-VALVE ENGINE; IT WAS RATHER AS IF IT HAD TWO COMBUSTION CHAMBERS WITH TWO VALVES EACH.

"IT FOLLOWED NATURALLY, THEREFORE, THAT THOSE FOUR-VALVE ENGINES SHOULD BE INFERIOR TO THE TWO-VALVE ENGINES BUILT IN THE SAME PERIOD. AND THEN CERTAIN TECHNICAL CHOICES, SUCH AS THAT OF ELECTRONIC FUEL INJECTION, WERE DETERMINED BY THE NEED TO BUILD AN ENGINE THAT WAS WELL-SUITED BOTH TO RACING AND ROAD USE.

"WE CHOSE ELECTRONIC INJECTION OVER THE MORE TRADITIONAL CARBURETOR SYSTEM BECAUSE OF THE REGULATIONS ADOPTED IN THE AMERICAN SUPERBIKE CHAMPIONSHIPS.

"IN FACT, THE REGULATIONS OF THE AMERICAN MOTORCYCLE ASSOCIATION (AMA), WHICH WERE THE FIRST REGULATIONS TO BE ADOPTED FOR THIS TYPE OF RACING, REQUIRED THAT THE SAME KIND OF CARBURETOR THAT WAS USED FOR THE PRODUCTION BIKE BE EMPLOYED ON THE RACING BIKE. THIS WAS AN APPROACH THAT WINDS UP HURTING ONE OF THE TWO BIKES, SINCE THE CARBURETION SYSTEM THAT WAS APPROPRIATE FOR THE ROAD BIKE IS INADEQUATE FOR THE RACING BIKE, AND VICE VERSA.

"WITH INJECTION, ON THE OTHER HAND, THESE PROBLEMS DISAPPEARED."

WITH THESE WORDS FROM MASSIMO BORDI, WE HAVE LEARNED THE BEHIND-THE-SCENES STORY, THE TRUE PROLOGUE TO THE PRODUCTION OF THE "DESMOQUATTRO" ENGINE.

NOW LET'S SEE HOW IDEAS AND PLANS MATERIALIZED IN THE MODELS THAT BROUGHT ABOUT THE GREAT REVOLUTION IN DUCATI PRODUCTION.

851 THE AGE OF THE SUPERBIKE BEGINS

The Ducati "Desmoquattro" series officially began with the Superbike 851. It was presented first in the racing version, indicated with the name 851 Superbike Kit, followed by the street version, called the 851 Superbike Strada. The year was 1988.

The two bikes are very similar, both in terms of engineering and styling. Indeed, except for turn-indicators and rear-view mirrors, you might say at a glance that the two motorcycles are identical. In technical terms, the only difference that meets the eye is the size of the wheels: 17-inch on the Kit and 16-inch on the Strada.

Both models went into production only a couple of years after Ducati set out upon the project described by Massimo Bordi in the introduction of this book. This was an important period, crucial to the success of the 851, and the period of gestation of the entire new family of Ducati Superbikes.

On these two pages, the 851 in its first incarnation of 1988, both in the Kit version and in the Strada version. On the right, the two motorcycles shown together, differing only by the Kit's lack of turn indicators. In terms of appearance, the differences are minimal, while in technical terms the most noticeable differences have to do with the diameter of the front wheel, which was 16 inches on the Strada and 17 inches on the Kit, and the exhaust. On the left, the Kit with the 1989 color scheme. Below, the Kit in action on the race track of Misano during the press presentation in the spring of 1988.

To understand more completely the development that led to the production of the 851, and the various processes of evolution it underwent, let us hear from Engineer Bordi once again.

"The first 'Desmoquattro' came out in 1986, and it was called the 748, which was, of course, the engine displacement. Our primary goal was to build a winning motorcycle. Its specifications were tested and fine-tuned, first on the racetrack, and then in the street. The initial interest

was in racing, and the bike was entrusted to Marco Lucchinelli, Virginio Ferrari, and Juan Garriga. It made its debut at the Bol d'Or.

"On the racetrack, honestly, Team Ducati must have seemed like so many Don Quixotes, chasing an impossible dream. Design had begun in January. By July the engine was already being bench-tested. The frame was ready in August, and by September the motorcycle was running on the track. Just try to imagine what this pace meant for a company like Ducati,

Left, the earliest version of the 851, photographed in the courtyard of the Ducati factory in the winter of 1988, immediately after it had come off the assembly line. With respect to the version that was later marketed, this "pre-series" version differs only in the color scheme, while the rest is the same. The engine, the frame, and the wheel mechanism had already been completely fine-tuned during the racing experience of 1987, when Ducati appeared at the starting line of the Italian Superbike championship with Marco Lucchinelli.

In the history of the Ducati Desmoquattro series, racing deserves a place of considerable importance. In fact, racing looms large both in the ties with Ducati tradition and in the technical development and engineering efforts which then led to the street models. On these pages, two of the racers that did most to make the Ducati name great, or let us say, to maintain the greatness of that name: Marco Lucchinelli, above and right, and Raymond Roche, below. After racing motorcycles against each other in the world championships, they found themselves on the same team but in different jobs: Roche striving to win the first world championship of his career, and "Lucky," team manager, in the effort to make the most prestigious win in Ducati's history. Both of them achieved their goals in 1990. After two years of striving to overtake Fred Merkel on his Honda RC 30, Roche gave Ducati its first world title in the Superbike class. And this success might well have been an even greater triumph had Giancarlo Falappa, the other "official" Ducati racer, not suffered an accident during the season.

producing in such a short time, and for the first time, both a completely new frame and a liquid-cooled, four-valve, fuel-injected Desmo engine. To give just one example, for the fuel injection we used the 'I.A.W. Alfa-N' system, which had been developed by Weber for the Ferrari F40. This was a system that was nicely suited for a supersport engine, or better yet, a racing engine like ours. The only modifications that we made were those that were absolutely necessary—they involved the butterfly valves. Everything else, including the injectors, was the same as in the F40. And thanks to Weber, who allowed us to rely on many of their technicians and engineers, in just a few months the mechanism had been adapted to the requirements of our engine.

"The race served as a true test bench, or track. The engine was not breathing right; the air intakes were inadequate, and we had a great number of problems. Perhaps everyone who was watching felt sorry for us, but that was the beginning of the great Ducati challenge.

"The displacement of the 'Desmoquattro' engine at the great debut was, as we have said, 748 cc. The ceiling of 851 cc, with which we began mass production in 1988, was reached soon thereafter. In fact, when we came back from the Bol d'Or, as disappointed as we were over the fact that we had had to withdraw, given the unreliable performance, and our embarrassment at being so badly outshone by the competition, we immediately set about solving the various problems. Indeed, because of the results obtained by the new four-valve engine, Engineer Taglioni decided that we should

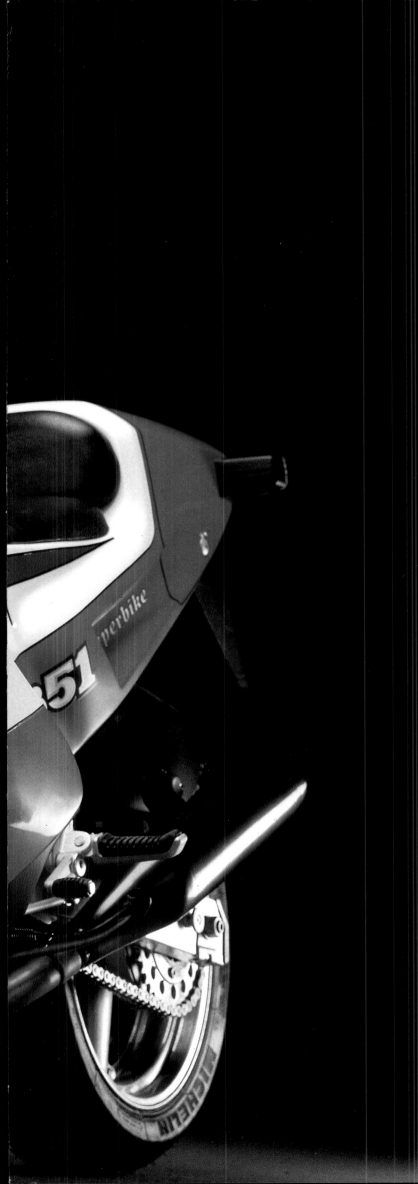

go back to work on the old two-valve engine.

"And so from September to December we made an attempt to improve the output of the Pantah power plant.

"From the initial 85 hp, we managed to crank up the output of the engine to 90 hp, in part through the use of a new air-intake manifold. We reached this 'ceiling' by raising the displacement to about 850 cc.

"The 5-hp improvement could certainly be considered a fine result, but it was simply not enough.

"In order to obtain optimal results, we had to increase the displacement of the 'Desmoquattro' to the level of the Pantah. Because of the increased bore of the 850 engine over the 750 engine, we could make use of flatter pistons, with a sharp improvement in the thermodynamics. Suffice it to say that from the initial 90 hp of the 748, when we increased the displacement to 851, we immediately reached a power yield of 115 hp.

"This was the turning point. I believe that the needle on the test bench of the Ducati company had never tipped past the threshold of 100 hp before.

"This increase in the displacement of the engine was an engineering decision, but it was partly determined by racing considerations, too.

"In 1987, the Italian Superbike Championships had already been established, with regulations for twin-cylinder engines that called for a maximum displacement of 1000 cc [instead of the 750 cc for multi-cylinder engines]. With the displacement of the 'Desmoquattro' raised to 851 cc, we

Just a few details should suffice to underscore the supersport nature of the 851 Superbike. The instrument panel is simple and spare with all of the instrumentation easy to read, even when traveling at high speeds. This is a feature that contrasts sharply with the hypertechnological instrument panels of Japanese bikes, but it is a fine piece of work that is eloquent in the tradition of Ducati. The instrumentation is mounted on a panel covered with polyurethane foam, which also contains the various warning lights.

Shown without fairing and superstructure, the 851 reveals its sharply designed latticework frame. This approach was prompted both by a desire to remain faithful to the Ducati tradition and by practical reasons. The simplicity of structure was combined with considerable rigidity (the flexing test is one degree per 200 kg.). The tubes, with a round cross section, were welded directly together, without the interlay of fine sheet metal. The engine hangs from the frame, but it performs a load-bearing function for the rear suspension, since the swingarm is hinged directly upon the crankcase. The rear framework was bolted directly to the latticework, and was made of steel tubes with a smaller cross section. Its purpose was to support the rear tail and the seat, as well as housing the battery and the electronic switchbox, which controls ignition and fuel-injection. The gray tube is made of plastic and it serves as an air manifold to the air intake box. The front end is distinguished by the Marzocchi fork, with 41.7-mm fork legs. It has adjustable anti-dive and spring preload. The Brembo floating double disks are clamped by four-piston calipers.

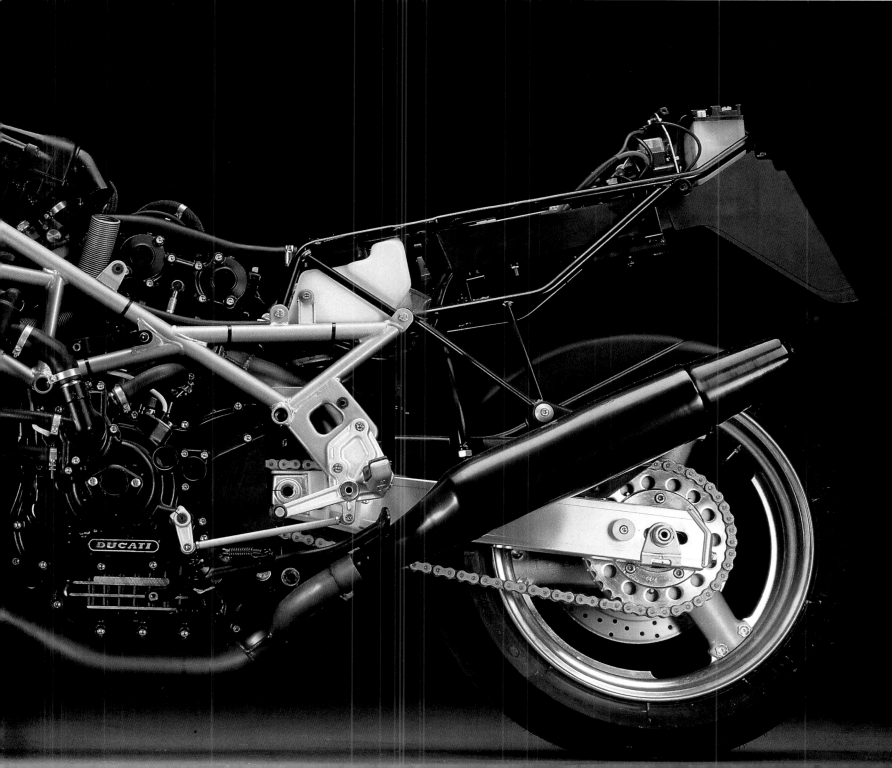

also began to see remarkable new levels of performance, though reliability was still not all it should be. Unlike what happened in later years, in 1987 the quest for reliability took second place, and was a secondary priority. Our determination to reach our goal was such that perhaps we can be forgiven for such an error."

It was an error that cost Ducati the Italian Superbike Championship in 1987. The skill and daring of Lucchinelli, combined with the 115 hp of the 851, to its 165 kilograms of weight, were not enough to outweigh the problems of reliability. Difficulties with the electronic fuel injection and damage to the connecting rod assembly prevented Lucchinelli on the Ducati 851 from succeeding against Fabrizio Pirovano on his Yamaha. This loss, however, did not stop Ducati's continuing development. In 1988, the 851 was ready for market, both in the Superbike Strada road version and in the Superbike Kit racing version. And it was the latter of the two that was first presented.

851 SUPERBIKE STRADA

The new superbike from Casa Ducati was a product of the race track, but it was not built for the race track. It was meant to offer its rider a strong array of sensations in terms of performance, braking, and safety, typical of a racing bike, while keeping in mind that it was aimed at a purchasing public of "road bikers."

Its exclusivity lay entirely in the conventionality of its engineering and styling decisions.

This may seem like a contradiction in terms, but it could hardly have been any different for a motorcycle that was meant not to betray its ties to the historic Ducati tradition. We have already heard about the principles that underlay this new bike—and it was precisely the adherence to those principles that made the 851 the forefather, so to speak, of that family that other motorcycle manufacturers have so envied and admired, without being able to imitate.

In comparison with the competition, the 851 appeared

less of a piece of design, at least in terms of line and finish, than others, and yet still possessed that charisma that so few motorcycles can boast; and it was more than simply the reflected luster of the achievements and victories of the Corsa, or racing version.

And yet, many were somewhat stumped when they first laid eyes on the 851: influenced by the reputation and achievements of the Corsa, they were often disappointed to discover that behind the Strada name was concealed a sport bike that was intended exclusively for use as a road bike.

The first model, the 1988, was not without its little faults, especially when you considered the price of close to 20 million Italian lire (to be exact, 19,796,000 lire, keys in hand).

Along with the finish, the main problems were with the riding position and the reactions of the chassis. The "triangle" of the seat-handlebars-footrest was not particularly comfortable, especially for tall people, while the

In 1989, Ducati seemed to be at a turning point with the 851, at least in the color scheme. The Desmoquattro series had taken on the personality that makes them unique and unmistakable bikes. The modifications did not end with the color scheme, however. It was especially the engineering differences that made the 851 a point of reference for the entire field of competitors. And all this without making any radical changes in the initial design. The fine tuning that emerged from the experience acquired during the races of the year were meant to give the street rider a bike with much the same handling and performance as the racing bike. In the wheel department, the most evident modification was that of using a 17-inch front wheel in place of the previous 16-inch wheel. The steering geometry too was modified, with the rake diminished by 3 degrees, shifting from 27 degrees 30 minutes to 24 degrees 30 minutes, while the trail was reduced to 94 mm from the 104 mm of the previous model.

In the power plant, which now had only one injector per cylinder, there was a slight increase in power, rising from 97 hp to 100 hp. The other changes had to do with the reduction in length and diameter of the inlets and the material of the intake valve guides. The engine's internal structure remained identical, with the same decidedly super-square measurements of the bore and stroke (92x64 mm). The crankshaft was made of forged steel with a single crank pin for the two connecting rods, which were also made of forged steel and cast in an "H" cross-section. The aluminum cylinders feature a nickel/silicon carbide facing, in order to lower friction.

16-inch front wheel had repercussions on handling and stability, especially on rough road surfaces.

These were minor "warts" of youth, not particularly serious when weighed against the performance and excitement that this motorcycle offered.

Prior to the debut of the 851, it seemed that a motorcycle engine's performance and power were proportionate to its displacement. It broke every rule and went against all logic to think that a twin-cylinder engine might have sharply superior efficiency to any multi-cylinder engine. And yet, in terms of speed, acceleration, and pick-up, the Ducati not only was able to hold its own against the various 750 cc four-cylinder bikes made in Japan, but it even distinguished itself in comparison with the ultrasports of 1000 or 1100 cc.

In addition to improved performance, electronic fuel injection played a role in limiting fuel consumption, too. With an average fuel efficiency of 16 kpl (kilometers per liter), the 851 Superbike showed itself to be one of the most economical big sportbikes to operate.

Statistics clearly show the quality of the engineering. The top speed was well over 230 km/h, and the bike took just over 11 seconds to cover 400 meters, from a standing start.

The suspension and the frame were both ideally suited to this level of performance, given that the components were the same as those used in the racing version.

The sensation of safety that came from the 280 mm Brembo twin floating disk brakes with four-piston calipers was reassuring, given the enormous power that the engine produced.

The only regrettable aspect was the selection of the 16-inch wheel instead of the 17-inch, as in the Kit version. The smaller wheel caused the bike to stand up under braking in curves. When the 851 Superbike Strada was presented and put on the market, the "Desmoquattro" project had already won great fame and popularity on the race track. The street version, nonetheless, would have won the same fame and popularity even if it had not enjoyed the "coattail-effect" of the racing model.

On these two pages, the 1988 851 Superbike Kit, above, and the 1989 851 Superbike Strada, left, in action.

The handling of these two motorcycles, despite their considerable differences in appearance, is quite similar, since many of the engineering solutions that were developed and applied to the 1988 Kit were then applied to the 1989 Strada. Thanks to the 17-inch wheel and the new steering geometry, the 851 became more precise in taking curves, and it lost the tendency to stand up under braking when the bike was leaned over. Contributing to this improvement was a better weight distribution of .

851 Superbike Strada 1988
Specifications

Engine: four-cycle, twin-cylinder "L" at 90 degrees with aluminum cylinders with silicon carbide facing. Liquid cooling, closed-circuit with radiator with thermostat. Bore and stroke: 92x64 mm Displacement: 851 cc. Compression ratio: 10.4 : 1 . Maximum power: 97 hp/EEC/shaft at 10,000 rpm. Timing: desmodromic with four valves per cylinder. Valve diameters: 32 mm intake, 28 mm exhaust. Lubrication: forced, with geared pump. Oil sump capacity: 4 liters. Fuel injection: electronic injection with two injectors per cylinder. Ignition: electronic. Transmission: primary with straight-tooth gearing, secondary by chain. Gears: 6 speeds. Clutch: multi-disk dry type with hydraulic control. Frame: tubular latticework made from chrome-molybdenum steel. Suspension: front, Marzocchi MIR fork, with 42 mm fork legs, 100 mm of stroke, and anti-dive regulated externally; rear, oscillating swing arm with two-setting Marzocchi shock-absorber, with stroke of 50 mm Wheels: Marvic, with magnesium spokes and aluminum rim, front, 3.50x16, rear, 5.00x16. Tires: Michelin tubeless radials, front A 59, 130/60 VR 16; rear M 59, 160/60 VR 16. Brakes: Brembo, front, two floating 280-mm.bimetal perforated disks with two-piston calipers; rear, floating 260-mm bimetal perforated disk. Wheelbase: 1,460 mm Max. length: 2,050 mm Height of seat: 760 mm Steering angle: 26 degrees. Trail: 105 mm Inclination of the steering column: 27 degrees 30 minutes. Fuel tank capacity: 20 liters. Dry weight: 185 kg.

Another double page devoted entirely to Marco Lucchinelli and Raymond Roche, riding the 851 and the 888. The displacement of the engine of the racing bike grew steadily from the initial size of 750 cc in 1986 to the 851 cc of the bike used in two successive seasons, and then up to the 888 cc of the version used from 1989 until 1992. Beginning in 1993, there was a further increase in engine size, first to 926 cc, and then to 955 cc.

851 SUPERBIKE KIT

The racing debut of the "Desmoquattro" series took place as early as 1986, as we have mentioned previously, but it was in 1988, when the first World Superbike Championship was run, that the 851 actually began to make news. The experience garnered in 1987 by Ducati and Lucchinelli during the Italian national championships gave them new prestige, and the first races in England, followed by the first race in Austria, gave them the air of contenders.

If the motorcycle of the year previous had tipped the needle on the test bench past the psychological watershed of 100 hp, the new motorcycle was still more powerful, producing 115 hp, and taking Lucchinelli to fifth place in the individual standings, and Ducati to fourth place in the manufacturer standingsp.

The process of fine-tuning had also resulted in a loss of some weight: from the 170 kilograms of the 750 that had run in the Bol d'Or, the 851 that ran in the world

championship weighed only 162 kilograms.

What Ducati lacked at this point, was total electronic and mechanical reliability in the 851, and total confidence in the bike's racing potential. The final results in the world championships could have been even better, if Team Ducati had decided to take part in the last two races in Australia and New Zealand.

Even before the Superbike world championships, the Ducati honor roll was lengthened with an unofficial second

On this page, a number of images from the 1989 racing season with Raymond Roche (numbers 31 and 27) and Baldassare Monti (29) racing for the world title. Roche took third in the world championship, while Monti took the Italian title.

This page, on the other hand, is entirely dedicated to Doug Polen in the 1991 race series. The American racer, shown racing in the unsuccessful, for him, Daytona 200 Mile Race, had no real rivals in his successful drive for the title, despite the fact that he was unfamiliar with the tracks of the world championship. His achievement was repeated the following year by the standard-bearer of Team Fast by Ferracci.

place by Stefano Caracchi in the "Battle of the Twin" in Daytona (unofficial in that Caracchi was not Team Ducati, but basically a private racer). Alongside its major racing challenges, the Kit began to enjoy successes in lesser competitions.

The motorcycle was made available to private citizens at a price of 23,460,000 Italian lire. That was a high price, admittedly, but it was competitive when one considers the overall cost of preparation kits to be applied to Japanese 750s. If we carefully consider the price of the Kit and compare it to the price of the Strada (19,796,000 Italian lire), we see that it was really not much higher, and we understand how similar the two versions really were; after all, the modifications were primarily in the regulation of the various components to satisfy the different operating conditions. In the engine, the main differences were in the

camshafts and in the calibration of the fuel-injection/ignition system; if we are looking for other differences, we must then turn to the exhaust, where the muffler terminals were replaced by "Corsa," or racing exhaust tubes. We should also look to the 17-inch wheels, instead of 16-inch, with slick tires instead of shaped treads. These are minor features, but they were enough to make the 851 Superbike Kit a true racing bike.

The power increased to reach the ceiling of 115 hp, while the maximum rpms rose to 10,500, as against the 10,200 of the Strada model. The year 1988 also proved to be an important one in terms of the fine-tuning and development of the entire "Desmoquattro" series—it was this experience that led to the 851's radical change, from 1989 on, of appearance, while still preserving the "heart" and the "soul" that made the Ducati name so great.

851 Superbike Kit

Specifications

The specifications are the same as those of the Strada version, with the following differences: Maximum power: 115 hp/EEC/shaft at 10,000 rpm. Wheels: Marvic, magnesium, front, 3.50x17, rear, 5.50x17. Tires: Michelin tubeless radials, front 12/60x17 slick, rear 18/67x17 slick. Dry weight: 175 kg.

Desmoquattro is both sport and production. The same motorcycle that tore around the race track, winning the 1990 Superbike world championship, with Raymond Roche (3), was available for normal street riding. The greatest differences between the two can be found in the functioning of certain minor details, but generally, the engineering is very similar between the two bikes.

851 SUPERBIKE STRADA 1989-90-91-92.

In terms of visual impact, this motorcycle was a completely different bike than the previous year's: the entirely red color pattern, contrasting with the white frame and wheels, made it even more aggressive-looking. It would almost seem that the new 851 was in no way related to the motorcycle of the year previous, even though they were very similar in technical terms. If the red-white-and-green coloring of the 1988 model might seem to have been chosen to give the bike an Italian identity on the world market, the colors chosen in 1989 clearly hinted at the race-track origins of this motorcycle.

What might have seemed like a slightly anonymous, even "timid" motorcycle, in terms of grabbing the attention of the public, was now an exuberant bike, busting out all over. Every motorcycle has a personality all its own, each model has its distinguishing features, but it was only now that the "Desmoquattro" underscored aesthetically those aspects that it had previously manifested in terms of power and performance.

After years in which Ducati had primarily been concerned with the substance of its motorcycles' performance, while completely overlooking their "looks," this time a successful

effort was made to amalgamate both aspects. Finally, the 851 was astonishing the world by its performance and by its line and appearance.

Alongside the aesthetic impact, the 1989 version was surprising in terms of price, too. Instead of increasing from year to year, as had been customary in the past, price decreased, considerably. It was established at 16,800,000 Italian lire, a drop of more than 3 million from the year previous. Even more surprising was the fact that the drop in price was not obtained through lower-quality materials or less exacting workmanship. In fact, the components were even finer, and the workmanship even more painstaking than before. In order to make the price more attractive, and especially more in line with the competition's supersports, an improved marketing approach had been developed. A greater number of models manufactured meant that there could be a greater amortization of fixed costs. And it had been the great success enjoyed by the previous model that had shown Ducati that they were on the right path, and that the market would accommodate a far greater number of bikes. A number of the "youthful shortcomings" of the first model had been solved, as well. The lattice-work frame had been preserved, but in order to improve the handling, the

bike's stability on bad surfaces, and the immediacy and accuracy of its response and handling, the steering geometry was changed and different-sized wheels were adopted. The angle of the steering shaft shifted from 27 degrees 30 inches to 24 degrees 30 inches, while the rake was reduced from 104 mm to 94 mm. The 16-inch wheels were replaced by 17-inch wheels. The tires, which were still Michelin radials, were now TXs, with a higher-performance profile than those of the A-M 59 series. And we find another new development on the wheels: the front 280-mm. double disk brake had been replaced by a 320-mm one. Some refinement was done on the suspension calibration, and the driving position was improved, as well. These modifications, verified and tested on the motorcycle of the year previous, enormously improved the great potential of the engine and frame. Unlike what had happened with the first 851, this time all of the features typical of a supersport were emphasized. All of those little hesitations in steering, all of those minor uncertainties that in the past had threatened to contaminate the enormous potential of the Ducati twin-cylinder, were finally overcome.

The final demonstration, however, that the 851 Superbike S (where S stood for Strada, or "road bike") had not been designed as a racing bike, or in any case as a track bike, can be seen in the modifications that were made to the power plant. The most notable changes affected the fuel system. One injector was used per cylinder, instead of the two that had been used in the past. Modifications were made in the

electronic "mapping" of the injection timing. Changes were made in the intake pipes, whose diameter was reduced from 28 to 27 mm. The length of the intake manifolds was shortened by about 20 mm, while the valve-guides were made of cast-iron, and the valve-stems were chrome plated.

The exhaust system too was improved; a new system, designed by Termignoni, replacing the previous Mototank systems.

Again, these refinements were designed to make an engine that had been designed and engineered for racing better suited for road use. Indeed, the goal had been solely that of obtaining the highest power at the lowest rpms. And Ducati did even better: the rpms declined while the maximum power yield increased. If the 1988 engine had been capable of producing 97 horsepower by EEC standards per shaft (expressed hereafter as hp/EEC/per shaft) at 10,000 rpm, the next year's model could produce an output of 100 hp/EEC/per shaft while the rotations dropped to 9,000 rpm.

The 1989 model's handling of the bike showed the results of the changes in the engine. The reduction in rpms at maximum power output ensured a more relaxed, less demanding motorcycle. The power output became "creamy" and gentle, and it almost seemed that the "limits" imposed by the very structure of the engine had been overcome. Still, the reader should never forget that this remained a cutting-edge twin-cylinder engine.

While acceleration and torque were unbeatable, we

cannot say the same about performance at low rpms. Up to rpms of about 3,000-3,500, the pickup can only be described as sluggish, as if the engine were not working correctly. However, once you get past 4,500 rpm, the engine revs in the most exciting way, pulling well past 9,000 and stopping only once it has reached the limit of 10,200, which is the last point before the limit switch kicks in.

The 851, despite the fact that it is a "maximum power" sports bike, remains a bike designed for use on the road. Thus, although performance and handling are fundamental considerations, the people at Ducati have not forgotten about comfort and the devices that can make this bike better to ride. Just consider the average consumption level

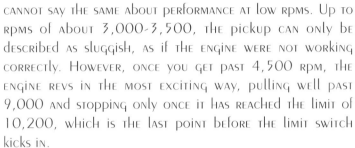

of about 17 kilometers per liter of gas, rising to a level of more than 20 kilometers per liter on the highway—clearly this is a motorcycle that has risen to a level of absolute international prominence for very good reasons.

The specifications of the 851, and especially the fact that its history and its development are directly tied to those of the racing model, might lead the reader to think of a rapid series of modifications and changes. Instead, due to the quality of the initial design, "Desmoquattro" production has been continuous since 1992.

Over the course of the years, the successive modifications that have been made since the 1989 version have been fairly limited in number, and always detail-oriented. In 1990, the most notable change was the

The pictures on these two pages show, and prove, the concept of the caption on page 37. This time the comparison is between the 851 Corsa, world champion in 1991 with Doug Polen, and the 851 Strada of the same year. If we leave aside the engine size, since the racing version already had the 888 cc engine, and the performance, you will find that these two are very similar motorcycles with the same engineering.

The development that was done on the racing models can also be found on the street versions. In the photograph on the left, is the 1991 851 Corsa (number 8) and in the shot on the right, is the 1989 version (9). All you need do is observe the height of the exhaust pipe, which is a fine indication of the lean angle you can assume on this bike, and you will see the remarkable increase in performance that has been attained. Also noteworthy is the increase in the number of body parts made of carbon fiber, and the replacement of the Marzocchi fork with an Öhlins unit, which offers far greater adjustment possibilities.

adoption of a two-person seat. In the engine, the Austrian Pankl connecting rods were replaced with billet Macchi connecting rods. The next year, the changes were far more substantive, though the overall specifications of the 851 did not change. The front mudguard was smaller in size, while the shape of the rear-view mirrors changed. Much criticism had been leveled at the round mirrors, especially with respect to appearance, and they were replaced by rectangular rear-view mirrors. The most important changes had to do with the suspension. The Marzocchi M1-R front fork was replaced with an upside-down Showa unit, and the rear shock absorbers, which were also Marzocchi, were replaced by Öhlins shocks. In both cases, the replacement components offered greater range in terms of adjustment. The front fork, which has fork legs with travel of 41 mm and 120 mm, adjustable for rebound, damping, and preload. The single shock absorber, which has a stroke of 65 mm. and 110 mm. of wheel travel, adjustable for rebound, damping, and preload. In the chassis there is also an increase of one millimeter in the rake from 94 to 95 mm, and the seat is slightly higher, rising from 760 to 790 mm, as did the footpegs, from 360 to 400 mm.

851 S 1989-90

Specifications

Engine: four-cycle, twin-cylinder "L" at 90 degrees with aluminum cylinders with silicon carbide facing. Liquid cooling, closed-circuit with radiator with thermostat. Bore and stroke: 92x64 mm Displacement: 851 cc. Compression ratio: 11:1. Maximum power: 100 hp/EEC/shaft at 9,000 rpm. Timing: desmodromic with four valves per cylinder and dual overhead cam shaft, driven by a toothed belt. Valve diameters: 32 mm intake, 28 mm exhaust. Lubrication: forced, with geared pump. Oil sump capacity: 4 kg. Fuel injection: Weber indirect electronic injection Alfa/N with one injector per cylinder. Ignition: electronic I.A.W. type with inductive discharge. Transmission: primary with straight-tooth gearing, secondary by chain. Gears: six speeds. Clutch: multi-disk dry type with hydraulic control. Frame: tubular latticework made from 25 Cr Mo 4 steel tubes. Suspension: front, Marzocchi MIR fork, with 41.7 mm fork legs, 100 mm of stroke, and anti-dive, regulated externally; rear, oscillating swing arm with Marzocchi single shock-absorber, with stroke of 65 mm and wheel travel of 110 mm Wheels: front, MT 3.50x17, rear, 5.50x17. Tires: Michelin Hi-Sport Radials, front 120/70 or 130/60x17, rear 180/55 or 180/60 or 170/60x17. Brakes: Brembo, front, 320-mm double disk with double-piston; rear, 245-mm. fixed disk. Wheelbase: 1,430 mm Max. length: 2,000 mm Height of seat: 760 mm Steering angle: 26 degrees. Trail: 94 mm Inclination of the steering column: 24 degrees 30 minutes. Fuel tank capacity: 20 liters. Dry weight: 190 kg. Average fuel consumption: 5.8 liters per 100 km. Top speed: 240 km/h.

NOTE

with unhampered exhaust, no intake filter, and the appropriate chip, the following performance is obtainable: Top speed of 250 km/h, Maximum power of 107 hp/EEC/shaft.

851 SUPERBIKE CORSA 1989

The year 1989 marked a two-fold development in Ducati racing production: the 851 logo remained, but the actual displacement rose to 888 cc, and alongside the Corsa model, which replaced the earlier Kit model, the SP model was introduced.

The production of the SP was justified by the rules of the Sport Production racing category. In 750 class racing, models equipped with twin-cylinder engines can compete even if the displacement of their engines is greater than 750 cc. On both versions, the displacement was increased through a 2-mm over-bore. The Corsa had reached its full racing maturity. Although the new Ducati star Raymond Roche was forced to yield to the greater experience of American racer Fred Merkel—who clinched his second consecutive World Superbike title—the Ducati proved that it was ready to go for the most prestigious award.

The team competing in the world championships was headed by Marco Lucchinelli, who still likes to ride every now and again both to test new engineering approaches, and to savor the thrill of racing. Luchinelli had to manage the skills of Roche and Baldassare Monti, two racers with diametrically opposed approaches, but both aggressive and uninhibited in their competition styles. Roche seemed to be in the last stretch of a career that had taken him onto the winner's platform in the world championship for 500 cc motorcycles, while "Sarre" Monti was a young racer who came up through Italian national championships and who was a European champion of the BOT, or Battle of the Twins. The two racers made perfect partners, and seemed to prove that Ducati was ready for the great race. The performance of Roche and Monti, especially at the end of the season, seemed to make it abundantly clear that the

reliability problems of the previous season were now entirely solved. Only the racing experience of Team Ducati seemed to be less than adequate; everything else, however, seemed ready to make Ducati the number one player in this category. The third-place taken by Roche and the eighth-place standing of Monti in the 1989 Superbike world championships made it clear that this was not a case of dumb luck; it had become clear that performance and reliability now went hand-in-hand at Ducati. It seemed that the fine-tuning of this motorcycle was now entirely complete. Power had increased to well over 130 hp, while the bike's weight, in racing form, had dropped to 158 kilograms. These were specifications that, while possibly not sufficient for victory in the world championship, allowed Monti to win the Italian national Superbike title.

851 Superbike Corsa 1989

Specifications

Engine: four-cycle, twin-cylinder "L" at 90 degrees with aluminum cylinders with silicon carbide facing. Liquid cooling, closed-circuit with radiator with thermostat. Bore and stroke: 94x64 mm Displacement: 888 cc. Compression ratio: 11.2:1 . Maximum power: 134 hp/EEC/shaft at 10,500 rpm. Maximum rpm: 11,000 rpm. Timing: dual overhead cam shaft, four valves per cylinder driven by a toothed belt, desmodromic system. Valve diameters: 33 mm intake, 29 mm exhaust. Lubrication: forced, with geared pump. Circuit capacity: 4 kg Fuel injection: Weber indirect electronic injection Alfa/N with two injectors per cylinder. Ignition: electronic I.A.W. type with inductive discharge. Transmission: primary with straight-tooth gearing, secondary by chain. Gears: six speeds. Clutch: multi-disk dry-type with hydraulic control. Frame: tubular latticework made from 25 Cr Mo 4 steel tubes. Suspension: front, Öhlins upside-down fork, with 41.7 mm fork legs, 100 mm of stroke, and anti-dive; rear, oscillating swingarm with progressive single shock-absorber, with stroke of 50 mm and wheel travel of 95 mm Wheels: MT, front 3.50x17, rear, 5.50x17. Tires: Michelin racing slicks, front 12/60-17, rear 18/67-17. Brakes: front, 320-mm double disk with 15-mm pump cylinder and 32-mm four-piston calipers, braking surface of 92 sq-cm; rear, 260-mm disk, with 11-mm pump cylinder and 32-mm caliper cylinder, braking surface of 25 sq-cm. Wheelbase: 1,425 mm Max. length: 1,995 mm Height of seat: 760 mm Rake: 125 mm Inclination of the steering column: 27 degrees 30 minutes. Fuel tank capacity: 20 liters. Dry weight: 155 kg.

851 SUPERBIKE SPORT PRODUCTION 1989-90

The winning quality of the "Desmoquattro" series has always been that of combining the characteristics of a street bike with those of a racing bike, and vice versa.

Until the production of the first SP version in 1989, however, there was always a sharp boundary between the motorcycle intended for the public and the bike used in races. It may not have been a particularly deep demarcation, but it was still there.

With the SP this differentiation vanished: without the slightest need for modifications, the same motorcycle could be run on the street and on the race-track. In the SP, the specific qualities of the Strada were merged with those of the Corsa: comfort, performance, and ease of use, all found together in the same motorcycle. This may seem like a pretty tall order to fill, but Ducati was already working from a high platform. All that was required was a refinement of the specifications of both versions, so that they could coexist without interference of any sort.

The first "Desmoquattro" that succeeded in combining the qualities of one and the other was the SP2 of 1990. The first SP version was really little more than a prototype, almost a reworking of the Strada. There was minor modification to the timing, with changes in the valve diameter and the breadth of the injection curve, permitting some increase in power. All the rest was virtually unchanged, however. Rather than a fully fledged new motorcycle, the SP of 1989 looked basically like a more-powerful version of the Strada. Things were entirely different in the next development, the SP2. Finally, you were looking at a model with a very specific technical and aesthetic personality. Compared with the other two models of "Desmoquattro" production, the SP2 is neither a "softer"

version of the one, nor a "wildcat" version of the other.

At first sight, the SP2 could be distinguished from the Corsa chiefly by its electrical system and by the aluminum mufflers in place of carbon-fiber mufflers. In comparison with the Strada, the most evident difference was the use of an upside-down fork. Clearly, however, the differences did not end here. The frame was the classic main latticework made of round tubing, with the rear seat support made of aluminum tubing. This version was clearly inspired by the Corsa model, since the Strada had all its tubing, and its entire frame, made of steel. The new developments in the rear were completed with the adoption of Öhlins shock absorbers, while both wheels and brakes were the same as those used on the street version.

The shock absorber allows 15 different settings, adjustable for rebound, damping, and preload. Far greater developments are found at the front end of the bike, even though the measurements of rake and inclination of the steering shaft were unchanged. The Marzocchi M1-R gave way to an Öhlins with upside-down fork legs allowing a broad span of adjustability, both in the hydraulic components and in the preload. Rebound is adjustable to 20 different settings, while the preload can be adjusted along a stroke of 18 mm. The possibilities thus become unlimited, offering optimal settings for facing any sort of road surface. Such a highly developed fork had never been used previously in a mass-produced street bike.

The braking system was absolutely unprecedented with comparison to the Strada model. It was also made up of a Brembo floating double disk, but with flanges in a light alloy and a cast-iron braking surface, instead of being made entirely of steel as had been the case in the past. The four-piston calipers, on the other hand, remained unchanged. The many

modifications in the chassis almost threatened to eclipse the changes made in the power plant. Like on the Corsa, the overall engine displacement was 888 cc. This increase was obtained through a 2-mm increase in the cylinder bore, a modification that you cannot see—the numbers stamped into the sides of the engine are still 851— but that you certainly can "feel." The claimed power was 116 hp, midway between the 100 hp of the Strada model and the 134 hp of the Corsa. In any case, it was certainly adequate to ensure a top speed of well over 250 km/h, declared officially by Ducati.

The new mechanical features of the power plant, in comparison with the engine of the Strada, did not end with the increase in displacement; they also concerned the timing, fuel injection, exhaust, and transmission.

The valves, both intake and exhaust, were larger in diameter by one millimeter. The intake valves thus grew from 32 mm to 33 mm, while the exhaust valves grew from 28 mm to 29 mm. The timing curve became broader, with the intake phase shifting from 261 degrees to 297 degrees, and the lift of the valves increased. There were changes in the manifolds, too. The intake pipes went from 27 mm to 28 mm, while the surface of the exhaust pipes was finished and no longer rough, as cast. The compression ratio increased too, shifting from 11 : 1 to 11.5 : 1. As far as fuel injection, exhaust, and the engine's internal components were concerned, the choices were the same as those made on the Racing version, or Corsa.

Weber indirect injection was used once again, with two injectors per cylinder, instead of a single injector. The exhaust system featured wider pipes, with diameters of 45 mm instead of 42 mm, and reverse-cone mufflers. In order to ensure greater reliability, Austrian Pankl connecting rods were used at first. These were used on early Strada versions as well. The

INCREASE IN POWER AND PERFORMANCE LED TO MODIFICATIONS IN THE GEAR RATIOS, WHILE THE CLUTCH WAS STRENGTHENED AS WELL. FOR BETTER HEAT DISSIPATION, THE COVER IS EXTENSIVELY PERFORATED (IT HAS A DRY CLUTCH). OIL IS COOLED BY ITS OWN RADIATOR.

IF WE ANALYZE THE MODIFICATIONS MADE TO THE SPORT PRODUCTION MODEL, WE CAN CLEARLY UNDERSTAND HOW ITS OPERATION WOULD BE OPTIMAL BOTH ON THE STREET AND ON THE TRACK. THE NATURE OF THE RIDE IS THE SAME AS THAT OF THE STRADA, BUT THE ENDLESS ARRAY OF POSSIBLE ADJUSTMENTS OF THE SUSPENSION AND THE STILL MORE POWERFUL AND SAFE BRAKING ENSURE A MORE ENJOYABLE RIDE.

AND ONE SHOULD NOT BE INTIMIDATED BY THE INCREASE IN PERFORMANCE. THE VERY STRUCTURE OF THE ENGINE MAKES IT CLEAR THAT IN ORDER TO GIVE ITS BEST, IT HAS TO "REV HIGH," BUT ONE SHOULD NOT BE SURPRISED AT THE FACT THAT THE THROTTLE RESPONSE AND TORQUE AT LOW RPMS ARE SUPERIOR TO THOSE OF THE STRADA. AND WHEN THE NEEDLE OF THE REVOLUTION COUNTER CLIMBS TO THE REGION OF 5,000 RPM, THE PROGRESSION OF THE DUCATI ENGINE TRULY BECOMES ASTONISHING. THOSE QUALITIES THAT ENSURED THE SUCCESS OF THE STRADA WERE NOW ENHANCED AND AMPLIFIED. AND THE SP2 WAS VICTORIOUS FOLLOWING ITS ENCOUNTER WITH ALL THOSE JAPANESE FOUR-CYLINDER 750s, RESULTING IN SUCCESSFUL SALES IN ITALY, AS IT HAD ALREADY ENJOYED ON THE INTERNATIONAL MARKET. CERTAINLY, THE PRODUCTION STATISTICS OF DUCATI COULD NOT VERY WELL BE COMPARED WITH THE STATISTICS FOR THE JAPANESE MANUFACTURERS, BUT IF YOU WANTED TO BUY AN 851, YOU HAD TO PUT YOUR NAME ON THE WAITING LIST, AND OFTEN YOU WOULD HAVE TO WAIT FOR NEXT YEAR'S MODEL.

851 SP2 1990

Specifications

ENGINE: four-cycle, twin-cylinder "L" at 90 degrees with aluminum cylinders with silicon carbide facing. Liquid cooling, closed-circuit with radiator with thermostat. BORE AND STROKE: 94x64 mm DISPLACEMENT: 888 cc. COMPRESSION RATIO: 11:1 . MAXIMUM POWER: 116 hp/EEC/shaft at 10,500 rpm. MAXIMUM RPM: 11,000. TIMING: dual overhead cam shaft, four valves per cylinder driven by a toothed belt, desmodromic system. VALVE DIAMETERS: 33 mm intake, 29 mm exhaust. TIMING DIAGRAM: intake open 44 degrees BTDC close 73 degrees BBDC EXHAUST open 77 degrees BBDC, close 42 degrees ATDC. LUBRICATION: forced, with geared pump, and with radiator on the lubrication circuit. CIRCUIT CAPACITY: 4 kg. FUEL INJECTION: Weber indirect electronic injection Alfa/N with two injectors per cylinder. IGNITION: electronic I.A.W. type with inductive discharge. TRANSMISSION: primary with straight-tooth gearing, secondary by chain. GEARS: six speeds. CLUTCH: multi-disk dry type with hydraulic control. FRAME: tubular lattice-work made from 25 Cr Mo 4 steel tubes. SUSPENSION: front, Öhlins upside-down fork, with 42 mm fork legs and 120 mm of wheel travel, adjustable for rebound and damping; rear, oscillating swingarm with progressive Öhlins single shock-absorber, with stroke of 65 mm and wheel travel of 110 mm. WHEELS: rims in light alloy, with three spokes, front 3.50x17, rear, 5.50x17. TIRES, front 120/70 ZR 17, rear 180/55 ZR 17. BRAKES: front, floating 320-mm double disk with four-piston calipers; rear, 245-mm disk. WHEELBASE: 1,430 mm. MAX. LENGTH: 2,000 mm. HEIGHT OF SEAT: 760 mm. STEERING ANGLE: 20 degrees. TRAIL: 94 mm. INCLINATION OF THE STEERING COLUMN: 24 degrees 30 minutes. FUEL TANK CAPACITY: 20 liters. DRY WEIGHT: 188 kg.

851 SUPERBIKE CORSA 1990

The year 1990 was an important one in the history of the Desmoquattro motorcycles: Raymond Roche, on an 851, took the title of world champion in the Superbike class. After two years of chasing after Fred Merkel on the Honda RC 30, the 851 showed that the choice of a twin-cylinder engine could result in the same level of performance as—if not even better than—the multicylinder engines. Ducati's success was even more significant, since at the head of the team was Marco Lucchinelli, this time wearing the hat of team manager. Lucchinelli is, of course, the same man who, as a racer, took the 851 on its debut spin. Roche's victory was the product of the perfect synchronization between the racer and the motorcycle's performance, as well as the French racer's enormous ability and skill, which he had so amply demonstrated when he was riding high-powered bikes in the world championships. But it was not Roche alone. The motorcycle also played a decisive part, with its performance and, in particular, with its reliability. Out of 26 races, Roche completed 24. One of the two forfeits took place in the final section of the New Zealand race when the title had already been awarded. And had it not been for the accident of Giancarlo Falappa, the second racer on the team, the results for Ducati would have been yet more impressive. Until the race

in Germany, the former motocross racer from Italy's Marche region had been one of the contenders in the championship, but a series of spills, beginning in Canada, and then with much more serious consequences in Austria, put an end to his driving ambition. His triumph in Great Britain, along with the eight race victories for Roche, confirmed the potential of the 851. The decision to take advantage of the opportunities offered by the technical rules, by increasing the displacement to 888 cc (94 x 66 mm), with a weight of only 146 kilograms, proved to be a successful one. Although the maximum power of the Ducati was slightly less than that produced by its competition—and we are talking about roughly 141 hp as compared with the range of 145-150 hp of the Japanese four-cylinder bikes—the weight-to-power ratio was still quite advantageous for the two-cylinder Bolognese bike. In comparison with the motorcycle that first hit the track at the Bol d'Or in 1986, giant steps had been made. The modifications which affected the intake and exhaust phases, the compression, and the cooling, were all aimed at obtaining that level of reliability that is essential to victory. And, just as was the case at the beginning of the Desmoquattro adventure, Engineer Bordi had seen very clearly which engineering decisions needed to be made, and the results leave no doubt about that.

On the facing page, the starting line of the 1990 Grand Prix of Canada at Mosport. In the front, you can see no fewer than three Ducatis. Giancarlo Falappa (6), who is starting in pole position, and, at his side, Raymond Roche (3), and the American racer, Jamie James. Completing the front line are the English racer Terry Rymer (7), riding a Yamaha, and the Belgian Stephane Mertens (2), with a Honda. Because Falappa took a spill during the race, Ducati had to "make do" with first and second place in both races, Roche arriving ahead of James both times. After Falappa's accident in Austria, James was drafted onto Team Ducati.

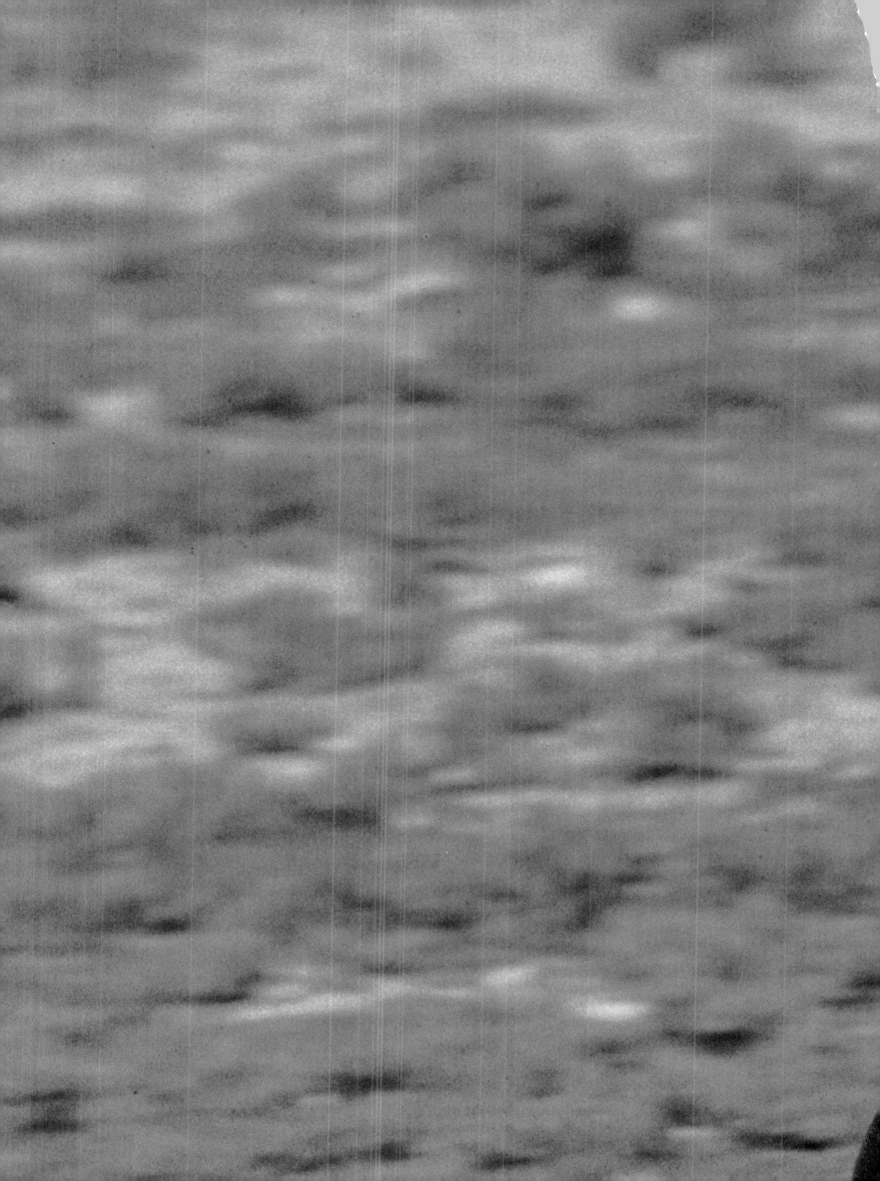

1991 851 S—851 SP3

Ducati was certainly not resting on the laurels of its world championship title of the year previous. And so, even if it was only on the racing version that the number 851 was replaced by 888 which indicated the actual displacement, both of the street models, the 851 S and the 851 SP3 were subject to a great many modifications.

We have already discussed the succession of modifications that were done on the 851 S with respect to the motorcycle that was presented in 1990, in the earlier chapter devoted to the street model of this motorcycle, while the SP3 represented the natural development of the previous SP2. In terms of aesthetics, the two bikes differ in their exhaust pipes, which were

851 Sport Production SP3 1991

Specifications

Engine: four-cycle, twin-cylinder "L" at 90 degrees with aluminum cylinders with silicon carbide facing. Liquid cooling, closed-circuit with radiator with thermostat. Bore and stroke: 94 x 64 mm. Displacement: 888 cc. Compression ratio: 11:1 . Maximum power: 116 hp/EEC/shaft at 10,500 rpm. Maximum rpm: 11,000. Timing: dual overhead cam shaft, four valves per cylinder driven by a toothed belt, desmodromic system. Valve diameters: 33 mm intake, 29 mm exhaust. Timing diagram: intake open 44 degrees BTDC, close 73 degrees ABDC; exhaust open 77 degrees BBDC, close 42 degrees ATDC Lubrication: forced, with geared pump, and cooling radiator on the circuit. Circuit capacity: 4 kg. Fuel injection: Weber indirect electronic injection Alfa/N with two injectors per cylinder. Ignition: electronic I.A.W. type with inductive discharge. Transmission: primary with straight-tooth gearing, secondary by chain. Gears: six speeds. Clutch: multi-disk dry type with hydraulic control. Frame: tubular latticework made from 25 Cr Mo 4 steel tubes. Suspension: front, Öhlins upside-down fork, with 42 mm fork legs and 120 mm of wheel travel, adjustable for rebound and damping; rear, oscillating swingarm with Öhlins single shock-absorber, , with stroke of 65 mm and wheel travel of 120 mm, adjustable for rebound, damping, and preload. Wheels: rims in light alloy, with three spokes, front 3.50 x 17, rear, 5.50 x 17. Tires, front 120/70 ZR 17 Michelin TX 21, rear 180/55 ZR 17 Michelin TX 23. Brakes: front, floating 320-mm. double disk with four piston calipers; rear, 245-mm. fixed disk. Wheelbase: 1430 mm Max. length: 2000 mm Height of seat: 760 mm Steering angle: 20 degrees. Trail: 94 mm Inclination of the steering column: 24 degrees 30'. Fuel tank capacity: 20 liters. Dry weight: 188 kg.

851 SUPERBIKE STRADA 1991

Specifications

ENGINE: four-cycle, twin-cylinder "L" at 90 degrees with aluminum cylinders with silicon carbide facing. Liquid cooling, closed-circuit with radiator with thermostat. Bore and stroke: 92x64 mm. Displacement: 851 cc. Compression ratio: 10.5:1. Maximum power: 100 hp/EEC/shaft at 9,000 rpm. Maximum rpm: 10,000. Timing: dual overhead cam shaft, four valves per cylinder driven by a toothed belt, desmodromic system. Valve diameters: 32 mm intake, 28 mm exhaust. Timing diagram: intake open 11 degrees ATDC, close 70 degrees ABDC; exhaust open 62 degrees BBDC, close 18 degrees ATDC. Lubrication: forced, with geared pump. Circuit capacity: 4 kg. Fuel injection: Weber indirect electronic injection Alfa/N with one injector per cylinder. Ignition: electronic I.A.W. type with inductive discharge. Transmission: primary with straight-tooth gearing, secondary by chain. Gears: six speeds. Clutch: multi-disk dry type with hydraulic control. Frame: tubular latticework made from 25 Cr Mo 4 steel tubes. Suspension: front, Showa upside-down fork, with 41 mm fork legs and 120 mm of wheel travel, adjustable for rebound and damping; rear, oscillating swingarm with Öhlins single shock-absorber, with stroke of 65 mm and wheel travel of 110 mm, adjustable for rebound, damping, and preload. Wheels: rims in light alloy, with three spokes, front 3.50x17, rear, 5.50x17. Tires, front 120/70 ZR 17 Michelin TX 21, rear 180/55 ZR 17 Michelin TX 23. Brakes: front, floating 320-mm. double disk with four piston calipers. Wheelbase: 1,430 mm Max. length: 2030 mm Height of seat: 790 mm Steering angle: 21 degrees. Trail: 95 mm. Inclination of the steering column: 24 degrees 30 minutes. Fuel tank capacity: 17 liters. Dry weight: 202 kg.

raised on the SP3; in the front mudguard, which was made of carbon fiber on the later model; and in the black wheels on the 1991 motorcycle.

In order to remove any lingering doubt concerning proper identification on both the SP2 and the SP3, there was a silver tag attached to the upper plate of the front fork, on which were inscribed the model number and the progressive numbering of the year of manufacture. And, of course, on the SP3, there was an indication of the world championship of the year previous. In all other ways, the motorcycles resembled each other, though a fine-tuning of the fuel-injection had improved the power yield of the engine. In any case, we are still talking about the exuberant performance of the 888 cc engine, which could propel this motorcycle at a top speed of over 250 km/h. And likewise the street performance remained similar; still, we should be thinking to track performance and a great chassis, when discussing the changes made to the SP2.

On the preceding pages, a number of images from the Ducati racing experience, culminating in the conquest of the first world title in 1990, by Raymond Roche. Out of the 26 races run, the French racer won eight, while one went to Giancarlo Falappa. Falappa, because of an accident in Austria, finished eleventh, right before Jamie James, the racer who replaced him.

In 1990, Ducati barely missed taking the world title for manufacturers and was beaten by just six points by Honda, 399 to 393.

888 CORSA

THE 888 COMES BACK FOR MORE

The impression of overwhelming superiority that was so clearly given in 1990 became even more unmistakable in 1991. Ducati won the title both for racers, with Doug Polen, and as a manufacturer. Ducati also finished second in the individual rankings, with the former world champion Raymond Roche. And, as if that had not been enough, Davide Tardozzi also won the European championship. For those interested in numbers and statistics, we should also mention that among the first four racers ranked in the world championship, three were riding Ducatis. Nineteen ninety-one was also an important year for the development of the Desmoquattro series. For the first time, the name 851 was replaced by the more accurate one of 888, which represented the actual engine displacement.–At the start of the world championships Ducati showed up with three teams: the "in-house" team led by the outgoing champion, Roche; the team promoted by Italian expatriate and tuner, Eraldo Ferracci, which featured Polen as rider; and a team operated by Stephane Mertens . In all three cases, the motorcycles were running officially and differed only in the rider set-up, and in the tires chosen by the racers themselves. (Roche chose Michelin tires, Polen Dunlops, and Mertens Pirellis.) Compared with 1990's bikes, the main equipment changes had to do with the exhaust system, the intake chamber, and efficacy of the air intake manifolds. This represented a process of fine-tuning which, when combined with the aerodynamic research, the weight distribution, and the improvement of the cooling system, yielded even more spectacular performance and greater reliability. The maximum power rose to more than 140 hp—official literature mentions 143 hp —while weight dropped to 143 kilograms. These results were obtained through the use of components made of carbon-fiber and Kevlar composites in the chassis, and the use of certain lighter components in the

In 1993, the racing career, at least the official one, of the 888 Corsa came to an end. It had begun in 1991, at least as a number used to identify the racing bikes, and under this number, Ducati took at least three world titles for manufacturers, two titles for racers, both with Doug Polen, and three final second-places, two with Raymond Roche and one with Carl Fogarty (4). In order to measure the superiority shown by the 888 Corsa, suffice it to add that in three racing seasons, it won in 63 of the 76 world championship races it ran.

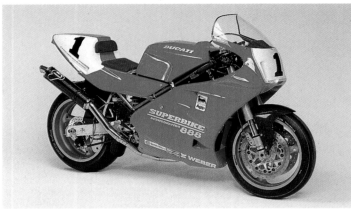

From top to bottom, three different versions of the 888. Top, the SP4 of 1992; middle, the 888 Racing of 1993; and bottom, the SP, 1993, aimed at the American market. The Racing is a racing bike sold to private racers, while the official version was called the Corsa. On the Racing, all of the technical solutions tested on the Corsa, the year previous, by the official Ducati racers, have been applied. Thus, private racers can purchase a true replica of the official racing bike.

engine itself, such as the drive shaft, the wrist pins, the flywheel, and the generator, and the pistons. None of these alterations undercut or distorted the technical specifications of the Desmoquattro series.

1992: THE 888 SPORT PRODUCTION DOUBLES ITS CHALLENGE

Production for 1992 was still focused on the 851 S, the more street-oriented version of the Desmoquattro (if you like, the less extreme model), while the SP range included two variants, the SP4 and the SPS (this last S standing for "Special"). The two SP models were exceedingly similar, and differed only in a few engineering and aesthetic details, and in their performance. Both were equipped with an 888 cc engine, but with a different fuel-injection mapping and a different valve diameter (both intake and exhaust). As a result, the engine of the SPS produced 10 hp more than the SP4, 126 hp against 116 hp. This increase in power affected the torque and the gear ratios, since the top speeds of the two motorcycles were practically the same. There was also a slight

888 SP4 1992
Specifications
The infomations in parentheses refers to the 888 SPS model

Engine: four-cycle, twin-cylinder "L" at 90 degrees. Liquid cooling, closed-circuit with 2.9 liter radiator with thermostat. Bore and stroke: 94x64 mm. Displacement: 888 cc. Compression ratio: 11:1. Maximum power: 116 hp/EEC/shaft at 10,500 rpm. (126 hp/EEC/shaft at 10,500 rpm). Maximum rpm: 11,000. Timing: dual overhead cam shaft, four valves per cylinder driven by a toothed belt, desmodromic system. Valve diameters: 33 mm (34 mm) intake, 29 mm (30 mm) exhaust. Timing diagram: intake open 44 degrees (53 degrees) BTDC, close 73 degrees (71 degrees) ABDC; exhaust open 77 degrees BBDC, close 42 degrees ATDC Lubrication: forced, with geared pump, and cooling radiator on the circuit. Circuit capacity: 4 kg. Fuel injection: Weber indirect electronic injection Alfa/N with two injectors per cylinder. Ignition: electronic I.A.W. type with inductive discharge. Transmission: primary with straight-tooth gearing, secondary by chain. Gears: six speeds. Clutch: multi-disk dry type with hydraulic control. Frame: tubular lattice-work made from 25 Cr Mo 4 steel tubes. Suspension: front, Öhlins upside-down fork, adjustable for rebound and damping, with 42 mm fork legs and 120 mm of wheel travel; rear, oscillating swingarm with Öhlins single shock-absorber, adjustable for rebound, damping, and preload, with wheel travel of 120 mm. Wheels: rims in light alloy, with three spokes, front 3.50x17, rear, 5.50x17. Tires, front 120/70 ZR 17 TX21 Michelin, rear 180/55 ZR 17 TX 23 Michelin. Brakes: front, floating 320-mm double disk with four-piston calipers; rear, 245-mm fixed disk. Wheelbase: 1,430 mm Max. length: 2000 mm. Height of seat: 760 mm. Steering angle: 20 degrees. Trail: 94 mm. Inclination of the steering column: 24 degrees 30 minutes. Fuel tank capacity: 17 liters. Dry weight: 188 kg (185).
Note: The SP has a steel fuel tank with a fuel pump and filter, incorporated inside. On the SP Special, the fuel pump is made of carbon fiber and Kevlar, with a new design, including front air inlets; easy removal fastenings, and a safety valve.

difference between the dry weights of the two motorcycles with the SPS tipping the scales at 185 kilograms, 3 kilograms less than the SP4.

In terms of equipment, the SPs were very similar differing

The 888 Strada (1994), the 888 SP5 (1993), and the 888 Racing (1994) show the three degrees of specialization of the Desmoquattro line. The differences are limited, and not only in the styling. All three models are manufactured according to the technical scheme that inspired the entire series of Ducati Superbikes.

The Racing, in comparison with the official Corsa, differs chiefly in that it has steel brake disks, not carbon.

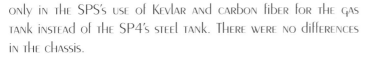

only in the SPS's use of Kevlar and carbon fiber for the gas tank instead of the SP4's steel tank. There were no differences in the chassis.

1992 888 CORSA: JUST LIKE BEFORE

No one ever questioned the fact that Ducati is a company attached to traditions, despite the manufacture of the various Desmoquattros, but no one expected so great an attachment to tradition that Ducati would present the same results at the races as it had the year previous. And yet, once again, for the third year running, Ducati won the racers' title, and for the second year running, took the title for manufacturers. And, as if these results were not enough to show Ducati's absolute loyalty to tradition, the European Superbike championship was taken by a Ducati, and—exactly as in 1991—the second- and fourth-place racers in the world championships were riding Ducatis.

Indeed, the first- and second-place winners in the world championship were the same as the first two of the previous season: Doug Polen and Raymond Roche. Fortunately, the name of the fourth-place winner had changed to Giancarlo Falappa, while Mertens, riding a Ducati, came in seventh. Behind him were two more Ducatis, one ridden by the European champion Daniel Amatrian, and the other by Carl Fogarty. Like the championship of the previous year, this was a race series that thrived on infighting among the various Ducati-mounted racers, though this year Polen was less of a towering victor. If in 1991 the American racer had thoroughly outclassed all his rivals no matter how ambitious, this time his victory was harder-won, and less of a sure thing. The role played by Ducati remained the same, however. Out of 26 races run, Ducati racers won 20.

The superiority of the Ducatis, in contrast with what one might reasonably expect, proved to be quite constructive for the future and the development of Superbikes themselves. The partial apathy of the Japanese manufacturers, which had come on the heels of their initial supremacy, begin to give way to new projects. Defeat always hurts, and when it is defeat at the hands of a manufacturer like Ducati, it leaves scars that don't quickly heal.

1993 888 SUPERBIKE STRADA

After five years of honorable, and even heroic, service, the 851 went into retirement. To tell the truth, it was a set of numbers that went into retirement, not a motorcycle, since the new 888 Superbike Strada was nothing other than an updated version of the well-known 851 S.

After several years on the cutting edge, and following a spectacular series of triumphs in many prestigious races, the Desmoquattro version of the 888 cc engine was now used on a model of bike that was more in the sport touring class—and touring with a passenger at that.

In aesthetic terms, the differences went beyond the numbers 888 in place of the old 851. The most noticeable changes were the fairing's appearance and its air intakes, the different gas tank and tail-section shapes, the color of the hubs (now black), and the bronze-colored frame.

The most important changes, however, had to do with the power plant and a new filter casing. The increased displacement made it possible to attain a maximum power rating of 104 hp. This result was designed to improve the

torque at low and medium revolutions. As compared with the engine that drove the 888 SP, from which the Strada engine was derived, this improvement was accomplished by changes to the injection system and the ignition timing . The valves were one millimeter smaller in diameter, and the peak revolutions dropped from 11,000 to 9,500 rpm.

What remained from the 851 S were the frame and the wheels. The front and rear Showa suspensions and the power of the Brembo braking systems remained unchanged. The handling and response of the two models were roughly comparable, even though the greater smoothness of the revised power plant allowed a more reasonable and less racy use of the bike. Top speed performance was greatly improved, however, now peaking at well over 250 km/h.

In line with the price of the 851 S, the 888 Superbike Strada was priced—as were all the Desmoquattros—to make it a truly exclusive piece of machinery. In 1993, the price had been set at 16,850,000 Italian lire, keys-in-hand, at the dealership. There were the added costs of

Two pictures of Carl Fogarty during the 1993 season, when the English racer was forced to make do with second-place, behind the American racer Scott Russell. Partial compensation for Fogarty, however, came from the fact that he had won twice as many races as his rival, ten against five, and that he helped Ducati win its third consecutive world manufacturers' title. That is a major achievement, once again indicating the quality of the motorcycle, and demonstrating that the first defeat in three years of absolute dominance in the racers category, was certainly not due to technical problems. Indeed, the Ducati loss triggered new interest in a championship that otherwise would have seemed to be under lock-and-key by the Bologna-based manufacturer. The victory of a Japanese manufacturer, and the direct involvement of all the other manufacturers, thus helped to make this Superbike competition a true alternative to the more conventional world championships.

888 SUPERBIKE STRADA 1993

Specifications

Engine: four-cycle, twin-cylinder "L" at 90 degrees. Liquid cooling, closed-circuit with 2.9 liter radiator with thermostat. Bore and stroke: 94 x 64 mm. Displacement: 888 cc. Compression ratio: 11:1 . Maximum power: 104 hp/EEC/shaft at 9,000 rpm . Timing: dual overhead cam shaft, four valves per cylinder driven by a toothed belt, desmodromic system. Valve diameters: 33 mm intake, 29 mm exhaust. Timing diagram: intake open 11 degrees BTDC, close 70 degrees ABDC; exhaust open 62 degrees BBDC, close 18 degrees ATDC. Lubrication: forced, with geared pump. Circuit capacity: 4 kg. Fuel injection: Weber indirect electronic injection Alfa/N with one injector per cylinder. Ignition: electronic I.A.W. type with inductive discharge. Transmission: primary with straight-tooth gearing, secondary by chain. Gears: six speeds. Clutch: multi-disk dry type with hydraulic control. Frame: tubular lattice-work made from 25 Cr Mo 4 steel. Suspension: front, Showa upside-down fork, adjustable for rebound, damping, and preload; 46 mm shafts with 120 mm stroke, adjustable rebound, with 41-mm fork legs and 120 mm of travel; rear, oscillating swingarm with Showa single shock-absorber, adjustable for rebound, damping, and preload, 65 mm stroke and wheel travel of 120 mm. Wheels: rims in light alloy, with three spokes, front 3.50x17, rear, 5.50x17. Tires, front 120/70 ZR 17 TX 11 Michelin, rear 180/55 ZR 17 TX 23 Michelin. Brakes: front, floating double disk; rear, 245-mm disk. Wheelbase: 1,430 mm. Max. length: 2040 mm. Height of seat: 805 mm Steering angle: 24 degrees. Trail: 100 mm. Inclination of the steering column: 24 degrees 30 minutes. Fuel tank capacity: 19 liters. Dry weight: 202 kg.
Note: The fuel tank, fairing, seat, and air intake housing are all made of a carbon-fiber/Kevlar composite material.

getting the bike on the road and a special tax for motorcycles with a high-power rating, so the ultimate price rose to 18,190,000 Italian lire. That was a lot of money, but the ratio of price and quality remained reasonable.

1993 888 CORSA

The superiority demonstrated during the previous season had laid to rest all doubts about the role that Ducati would play in the 1993 championships, just as there was little doubt about

On this page, left, Carl Fogarty, below, Giancarlo Falappa, shown during the Grand Prix of England in 1993. During that season, Falappa took fifth-place, and won six races. On the double-page spread preceding, the 888 Corsa of 1993 ridden by Juan Garriga. Alongside the refinements in components, there was a notable increase of displacement, to 926 cc, although the bike continued to be identified as an 888; the power output also increased, grazing the level of 150 hp.

who the primary rivals would be. A certain thirst for revenge had been shown by the Japanese manufacturers, especially Kawasaki back in the 1992 championships. Still, nobody expected to find them as well prepared and as evidently out for blood as they were at the beginning of the sixth Superbike World Championship races. On the other hand, Ducati seemed willing and able to do without the two racers that had earned three world championships in the recent past. Two-time champion Polen was shunted off toward the American Superbike championship, while Roche decided to hang up his helmet, to take up a career as team manager.

Carl Fogarty and Juan Garriga, the two racers summoned to replace them, seemed capable of filling the former champions' shoes admirably. Fogarty had already won three world championships, in Formula 1 and Endurance, while Garriga was the veteran of a long career in world championship racing, first on 250s and later on 500s. Supporting them ably were the returning stalwarts, Falappa and Mertens. There was something new about the bike as well: the displacement had climbed to 926 cc, the result of a bore and stroke of 96x64 mm. The increase in displacement was matched by an increase in horsepower, now at 147, as against the 141 hp of the previous 888.

Right from the very first minutes of the championship, it was clear that the Japanese were not willing to make way for Ducati. The engineering superiority and the human skills and determination that had been amply demonstrated in the past ran up against a motorcycle, the Kawasaki ZXR 750, and a racer, Scott Russell, that were clearly driving for the title with absolutely no intention of giving quarter.

It wasn't long before the championship had become one long and continuous skirmish between Fogarty and the outgoing American Superbike champion. The duel was an exciting one. In the early part of the season, it seemed that Falappa might be about to enter the competition, but in the second half his performance varied too wildly to cause concern for the leading pair. Equally unable to break ranks was Aaron Slight, Russell's Kawasaki teammate. The way results stood at just two races short of the end, anything could still have happened between Russell and Fogarty. Fogarty pulled out all the stops at the Grand Prix of Great Britain (his home track) but made fatal errors, allowing Russell to win both races. The Englishman had to make do with a second place and a fall. For Russell and Kawasaki, the job was done: in the last race, in Portugal, they even withdrew from the race with a clutch failure. And Fogarty was only able to produce a win and another spill. Fogarty was beaten, but Ducati still had reason to celebrate—it had won another manufacturer's title.

That was a great result, but it left a bitter taste for those who had by now become accustomed to winning always. 916

916
DESMOQUATTRO

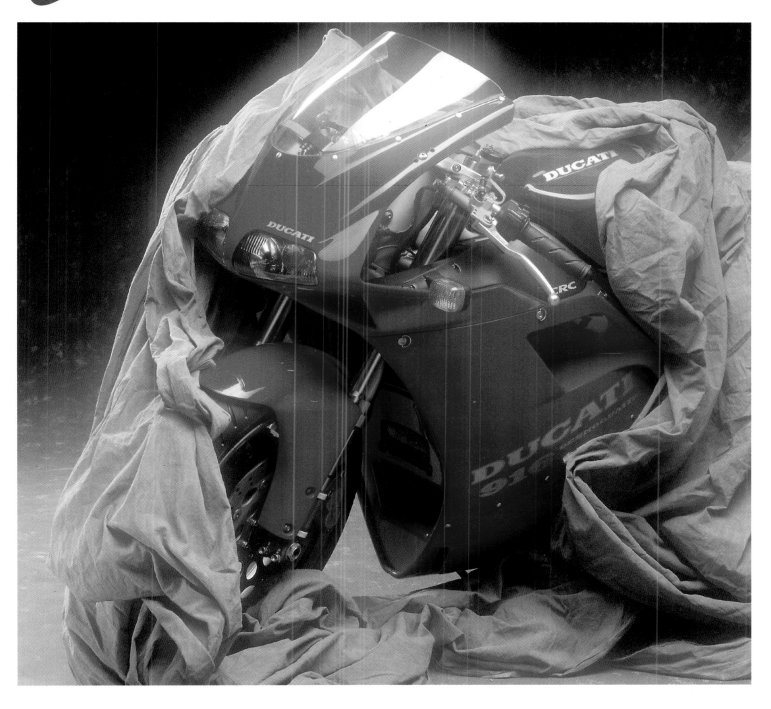

1994 916 DESMOQUATTRO

"For awhile, the Japanese manufacturers neglected the Superbike championship, but when they noticed the huge excitement that was being generated by Ducati and its victories, they went back to work on their four-cylinder bikes. And so, to meet the challenge of the heightened performance of their bikes, we progressively increased our engine size. We started with the 851, then went on to the 888, and then on up to 926, finally 955, and next will come the 1000. It is racing, with its growing demand for power and maximum performance, that determines the engine size of our motorcycles. For street riding, there was all the horsepower needed even in the earliest bikes. But, in order to justify the modifications added over time to the mass-produced bikes as well, you must not overlook the commercial effects that derive from operations of this sort." These words are from Engineer Bordi, who is our guide in this tour of the Desmoquattro universe; he is helping us to understand how and why in late 1993, the 916 came to join the great family of Ducati Superbikes. The defeat suffered by the 888 in the Superbike world championships of 1993, however, should not mislead the reader. The 916 project was already underway well before Carl Fogarty took what looked like an innocuous little spill at the Estoril, thus destroying all hope of giving Ducati its fourth consecutive world title. Indeed, it is reasonable to think that yet another victory for the 888 would have led the people at Ducati to rethink its retirement, considering that it had several good years in it yet. And when the 916 was

The 916, as you can see from the picture above of the frame, and the other shot, below, of the engine without fairing and superstructure, remains faithful to the engineering principle that inspired the Desmoquattro series. The frame presents the possibility of adjusting the steering head angle without altering the wheelbase, and also features a single-sided swing arm. A steering damper is located behind the steering collar, and transverse to the axis of the motorcycle.

presented, the 888 was enjoying solid commercial success still.

The 916 took up the basic idea of the 888, which underlay all of the series of Desmoquattro models: a motorcycle capable of merging, without loss on either side, the specifications of street supersport with those of racing bike. In comparison with the 888, however, and all the other versions of the Desmoquattro series, the 916 was an entirely unprecedented motorcycle. If with all of the previous models, we spoke of a succession of updates and refinements, the technical and aesthetic specifications and qualities of the 916 are such that we should truly speak of a new model, not a new version of

The major new technical developments of the 916 have done little to disturb its racing performance.

Carl Fogarty encountered no difficulty in adapting his style to the demands of the new frame. Following the line of development traced by the engine, with displacement climbing first to 888 and then to 926 cc, in the racing bikes, the 916 emblazoned on the motorcycle that Fogarty rides to a world championship conceals a 955 cc engine, with 150 hp maximum power.

the 888. In this context, the only points of contact between the two motorcycles are represented by the general architecture of the power plant, the timing, and the electronic fuel-injection. With the 916, Ducati was taking a further step forward in terms of research and state-of-the-art technology.

After having been concerned for a number of years only with the substantive aspects of the motorcycle, Ducati finally coordinated looks and performance in the design of the 916. If the 851 and the 888 had the unmistakable lines of a "racing replica," the 916 added a design and styling that combined the spare appearance of a racing bike with the beauty of a true "queen of the road." The frame maintained the traditional lattice structure, and to ensure the greatest resistance to twisting and flexing, the frame was constructed with round tubes made from 25 Cromoly 4 steel with three anchor points for the engine. To ensure even greater rigidity, an overhead panel was screwed to the upper side of the lattice-work structure. This panel also serves as an air box, and is an integral body component. For the first time an adjustment mechanism was installed to vary the angle of the rake. Two different positions, 24 degrees and 25 degrees, with accompanying variation of the trail, which shifts from 94 mm to 100 mm. This in no way interferes with the wheelbase, however. Indeed, this patented mechanism allows you to vary the rake without changing the wheelbase, by means of ellipsoidal bearings in the head tube. This device finds its most useful application in racing, but it was maintained on the street version as well in order to comply with the idea that all of the various Desmoquattro models are similar to each other, whatever the use to which they are put.

Also new to the Ducati manufacturing tradition is the

916's single-sided swingarm. Designed by computer, like the frame, it is the result of collaboration between the designers in the Centro Ricerche Cagiva and the racing division of Cagiva.

This is a differentiated cross-section single-sided swingarm, chill-cast from an aluminum alloy.

The efforts to fine tune the chassis affected the front and rear suspension systems as well. Both the fork and the single rear shock-absorber were changed from the ones used on the 888. The fork is still an upside-down Showa unit, but the version used on the 916 has 43-mm fork legs and allows 120 mm of wheel travel. The front forks

are adjustable for rebound, damping, and preload. Great care was devoted to the design of the triple clamps, which are processed in pairs in order to ensure the greatest possible precision. Extreme rigidity in ensured by the distance between the anchor points between fork and plates, and the base of the triple tree, chill-cast in aluminum alloy, has a distinctive "bridge" shape. The underside of the arch, moreover, serves to channel air to the radiator.

For the first time a steering damper was applied to the front fork. This solution was entirely exclusive, and like the single-sided swingarm and the adjustable front fork, was patented by Ducati. The steering damper was positioned transverse to the motorcycle's axis, behind the steering column, a position that assured total neutrality in response, since it affects the steering action symmetrically. Moreover, since it is extremely accessible, it can be adjusted while the motorcycle is in use.

Particular attention was also devoted to the rear unit, made by Showa, to make it as broadly functional as possible. In order to render very smooth operation, the entire rear suspension mechanism was fitted with Teflon lined steel spherical joints.

In order to round out the modifications made to the chassis of the 916 as compared with the 888, all that is left to describe are the wheels themselves, since the brakes were the only component left unchanged. The wheels still feature three hollow elliptical spokes with variable cross-sections. The attachment system was changed, necessarily for the rear wheel.

The rear wheel was keyed onto the journal by a single, large, central nut, while the journal itself was attached to the swingarm by an eccentric hub, making it possible to adjust the chain.

In such a general overhaul, there would simply have to be an equal degree of fine-tuning to the power plant. Since the increase in displacement clearly led to a notable increase in maximum power (109 hp at 9,000 rpm), the most work was done to improve performance throughout the range of use. In order to achieve this, the staff working under Engineer Bordi worked in a number of different directions.

These ranged from the increase in displacement (obtained by increasing the stroke 2 mm) to improvements in the intake and exhaust systems, in order to increase power at high and extended rpm. The 916's air intake is regulated by a sealed air box, with ram intake and filters in the ducts. The exhaust system is new, with pipes that follow the outline of the engine, then join beneath the swingarm, and finally rise separately to the mufflers partly covered by the tail section. This solution is not only quite effective in terms of aerodynamic penetration and handsome to behold, but also convenient for work on the rear wheel.

The increase in power also made it necessary to redesign the cooling system and the lubrication system. The water radiator has a 6 percent larger surface area than that of

916 DESMOQUATTRO 1994

Specifications

The informations in parentheses refers to the 916 SP model

Engine: four-cycle, twin-cylinder "L" at 90 degrees with aluminum cylinders with silicon carbide facing. Liquid cooling, closed-circuit with curved radiator with thermostat. Bore and stroke: 94x66 mm. Displacement: 916 cc. Compression ratio: 11:1 (11.2:1). Maximum power: 109 hp/EEC/shaft at 9,000 rpm. (126 hp/EEC/shaft at 10,500 rpm). Maximum rpm: 10,000. Timing: dual overhead cam shaft, four valves per cylinder driven by a toothed belt, desmodromic system. Valve diameters: 33 mm (34 mm) intake, 29 mm (30 mm). exhaust. Timing diagram: intake open 11 degrees (53 degrees) BTDC, close 70 degrees (21 degrees) ABDC; exhaust open 62 degrees (77 degrees) BBDC, close 18 degrees (42 degrees) ATDC. Lubrication: forced, with geared pump, with radiator on the circuit. Circuit capacity: 4 kg. Fuel injection: Weber indirect electronic injection Alfa/N with one injector per cylinder (Alfa/N type with two injectors per cylinder). Ignition: electronic I.A.W. type with inductive discharge. Transmission: primary with straight-tooth gearing, secondary by chain. Gears: 6 speeds. Clutch: multi-disk dry type with hydraulic control. Frame: tubular latticework, with an overhead cage, made from 25 Cr Mo 4 steel tubes. Suspension: front, Showa upside-down fork, with 43 mm fork legs and 120 mm of wheel travel, adjustable for rebound and damping, and for preload; rear, oscillating swingarm with Showa (Öhlins) single shock-absorber, with stroke of 71 mm and wheel travel of 130 mm, adjustable for rebound, damping, and preload. Wheels: rims in light alloy, with three spokes, front 3.50x17, rear, 5.50x17. Tires, front 120/70-17, rear 190/50-17. Brakes: front, 320-mm double disk (double cast-iron disk) with four differentiated pistons; rear, 220-mm disk. Wheelbase: 1,410 mm Max. length: 2,050 mm Height of seat: 790 mm Steering angle: 27 degrees. Trail: 94-100 mm. Inclination of the steering column, adjustable to two positions: 23 degrees 30 minutes(24 degrees) 24 degrees 30 minutes (25 degrees). Fuel tank capacity: 17 liters. Dry weight: 195 kg. (ready to ride, but without fuel).

The 916, right, is produced in an
SP version. As with its
counterparts, the 851 and the
888, this motorcycle blends racing
requirements with the demands of a
sporty tourister.

It is practically a blend between the
Strada and the Corsa, as you can
tell from the maximum power of
126 hp, instead of the 109 of the
Strada or the 150 of the Corsa,
or Racing version.

Below, and on the facing page, two
pictures of Carl Fogarty in 1994.
In the following pages, the 916 SP,
and then the 916 SP together with
the 916 and the 748 Biposto, the
three mainstays of Ducati's
Desmoquattro production in
1995.

the 888, and the route of the lines linking engine to radiator and radiator to expansion valve was reoriented. The thermostat valve and the cover of the pump set on the engine were also redesigned. In order to keep the temperature of the lubrication system constant, an oil cooler was built into the circuit, thus applying to the 916 road bike a solution that was previously found only on the Sports Production versions. Alongside the more obvious modifications, there are other changes such as a new gear system for locating neutral and a more powerful alternator. These changes primarily affect the motorcycle's usability and reliability.

As long as the engineering was being refined, Ducati could hardly help but improve the components and, of course, the appearance of the bike. Indeed, for the first time, great attention was focused on the appearance, in response to a long series of criticisms that had been leveled in the past. It is true enough that both 851 and 888 had their own distinct personalities, and that their race-track image prompted admiration, but theirs was also a fairly stark appearance that often contrasted with their class and, above all, with their very high sticker price.

With the 916, Ducati took a new direction in design. Just look at the twin-beam, poly-ellipsoidal headlight unit; the shape of the fairing; the new instrument panel and switches; and the handlebar and foot controls, and you will quickly see the care that went into the design of this motorcycle.

Power, precise handling, and breathtaking performance

are no longer enough to make a motorcycle "great."

With the 916, Ducati overcame the last gap that separated it from its competition. If the 851 and the 888 are striking chiefly for their race-bred allure, the 916 combines line and design to make it a new point of reference in the motorcycle universe.

DESMOQUATTRO 916 S.P. 1994

With the 916, the series of Sport Production versions continues. And, as was already the case with the various past S.P. models, the 916 S.P. also has a very specific role, with technical and aesthetic qualities that set it aside from the Biposto.

Like all the Desmoquattro machines that are also meant for racing, this one is equipped with a fuel injection system with two injectors per cylinder.

Modifications are also found in the timing system, both in the 1-mm increase in the size of the intake and exhaust valves, 33 to 34 and 29 to 30 respectively, and in the different ignition timing curve.

The modifications made in the power plant result in a considerable increase in maximum power, increasing from 109 hp at 9,000 rpm to 126 hp at 10,5000 rpm, giving the bike a top speed of 270 km/h. The tradition of having certain of the components made of carbon fiber in the S.P. versions was respected in the 916, as well. This material was used for the chain-guard, the housing of the rear brake line, the insulation panel for the exhaust pipes, the license-plate holder, the front fender, the front fairing section, and the mufflers.

On this double page, the technical details of the 1994 916 Corsa are "laid bare."

The motorcycle is the one ridden by Giancarlo Falappa, exactly identical with the world championship bike ridden by Carl Fogarty. To limit the weight, extensive use was made of carbon-Kevlar blend components, such as the front brake disks. This solution however was no longer used from 1995 on, as it was forbidden by Superbike technical regulations. In the case of Ducati, at any rate, it was superfluous, since the lowest weight allowed for twin-cylinder motorcycles was set first at 147 kg and later, when the season had begun, at 155 kg.

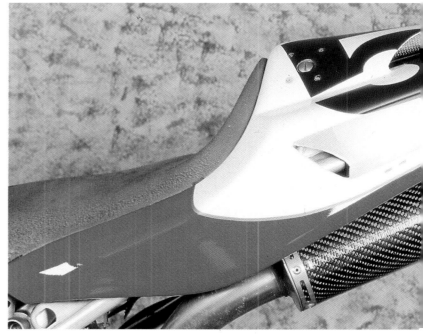

DESMOQUATTRO
916 BIPOSTO AND S.P.
1995

The first version of the 916, presented in 1994, is available only in a single-seat version.

This is a feature that makes this bike very similar to the S.P. of the same year—differences there may be, such as one as opposed to two injectors per cylinder.

But it was only from 1995 on that the 916 became available in a version suited for carrying a second rider. The Biposto, as this new two-rider version was named, offers the same equipment as the motorcycle of the year before, but with small changes, both in terms of appearance and engineering.

The most evident changes, given the Biposto name (which is Italian for "two-seater"), have to do with the seat, which extends back over the tail section. Supports and foot pegs for the passenger, and a small steel rear framework were also added. The presence of foot pegs for the passenger also required lengthening the chain guard for greater safety.

Technical improvements were also made, including molded connecting rods were used, the controller computer for the injection system was the new "1.6M" type, the frame has been reinforced, and the electrical system has hermetically sealed relays.

The calibration of the Showa single rear shock-absorber was also modified.

The modifications did NOT affect power and performance, which remain unchanged from 1994.

In 1995, the S.P. was updated as well. The brake lines were changed to braided stainless steel, and the frame was reinforced. As with the Biposto, the electrical system and relays were hermetically sealed.

The S.P. was equipped with a number of carbon fiber components such as the chain-guard, the housing of the rear brake line, the license-plate holder, the front fender, and the front section of the fairing.

The carbon fiber mufflers, on the other hand, were standard features.

In the case of the S.P., the power and performance remained the same as the year previous.

Again, an overall view: large shot, of the 916 Biposto, left; the 916 SP, center; and the 748 Biposto, right.

The other photographs on this page are of the 916 Biposto.

As you can see from the close-ups, enormous care is taken in tending to details. Along with the amazing performance and brilliant engineering, such as the frame with a single-sided swingarm and the adjustable inclination of the triple tree, new attention has been lavished on the styling, helping to make the Desmoquattro series an enormous commercial success in the Nineties.

1994 DESMOQUATTRO 916 CORSA

As we have already seen with the 851, the model number does not always identify the precise engine displacement. In fact, just as the 888 made its racing debut with the 851 model number, the same happened with the 916 Corsa, which "concealed" a power plant which had been increased in size to 955 cc. By increasing the stroke 2 mm, the 916 constituted the next step in the development of the 888, in the same manner the engine of the 955 was obtained by increasing the bore of the 916 by 2 mm. This increase translated into power of 150 hp at 11,500 rpms, especially useful in the world championship which was taken by Carl Fogarty in 1994.

This was a success that paid back Ducati and the English racer for the harsh defeat of the year before, reconfirming the capabilities of the twin-cylinder engine—against other multicylinder engines. The 916 Corsa—if we leave aside the increase in engine size, the carbon-fiber and Kevlar composites body components, , and a different fork—was entirely similar to the 916 Biposto. Even if we mean the factory motorcycle when we speak of the Corsa, the components were the same as those used on the street bike. A mix of carbon-fiber and Kevlar were used in manufacturing the gas tank, fairing, fenders, seat, and airbox. The fork, on the other hand, is by Öhlins, instead of a Showa, and has 46-mm fork legs instead of 43-mm ones. The use of ultralight materials made it possible to push the weight down to 148 kilograms, greatly improving handling and performance. This was the motorcycle with which Ducati answered the challenge of the Japanese. Kawasaki, Honda, and Yamaha had all stated that they were determined to reconquer a category which was now ruled by Ducati. Kawasaki had to prove that it earned its victory in 1993, while Honda, with a new model, hoped to regain the level of superiority it showed in the first races of the Superbike world championship. Yamaha was seeking a prestigious win that so far had eluded its grasp. In order to erase the humiliation of the loss of the previous year, Ducati presented itself with a new 916 and a new, stronger team.

Alongside Fogarty and Falappa, we thus found others straddling the Bologna-built twin-cylinder bike: Fabrizio Pirovano, Australian racer Troy Corser, and English racer Jamie Whitham, as well as a number of high-tone private racers, such as the Austrian Andreas Meklau and the Belgian Stephane Mertens, whose teams enjoyed supplies of special parts from Ducati so that their motorcycles were every bit as good as the official racing bikes. In terms of factory bikes, like the year before, there was a distinction between the "in-house" team, led by Virginio Ferrari and comprising Fogarty and Falappa, and the other teams. The quality and virtuosity of the racers were unquestioned, but doubts still existed concerning Ducati's chances of regaining the world title, and those doubts would hover until the mystery of the 916 was cleared up. The tradition of competitiveness, which began with the 851 and continued with the 888, was no longer enough. The 916 was a motorcycle with no history, having just had its racing debut, and it would have to prove that it was capable of upholding and rejuvenating the tradition inaugurated by the models that went before it. While the times set during the winter tests were taken with a grain of salt, the real first test was thought to be at the track where the world championship races would be starting, in the Grand Prix of England. Thus, the track of Donington, where Fogarty the year previous had seen his chances of winning the world title evaporate, would be the first acid test of the season.

The 916 immediately swept away all doubts about its capacity to compete: Fogarty got the highest points of the day, though Falappa, Pirovano, and Corser also demonstrated the solid work done by the Ducati technicians.

This photograph of a Ducati with the Cagiva name behind it symbolizes nicely the commercial and technical renaissance of this Bologna-based company. It was precisely because of its entrance into the Cagiva Group that Ducati was able to develop the entire Desmoquattro series.

On the facing page, left, the front end of the 916, with upside-down fork and carbon-fiber mudguard. On the right, the rear end with the single-sided swingarm and raised exhaust.

The Ducati 916 possessed a large engine (955 cc, despite the name); the chassis still needed some perfecting, though. It was in this first race at Donington, however, that it became clear that this was not going to be such an easy season. Both Kawasaki and Honda were running at extremely competitive levels. And it seemed that these formidable adversaries were going to be helped by the masochism of the Ducati racers. In the following race, in Germany, Fogarty was knocked out of the running right at the beginning, breaking his arm in a spill, while Pirovano and Falappa actually collided during the first race and were forced to retire. The second-place finish of Pirovano and the fourth-place finish of Falappa in the next race served to reconfirm that they were racing on competitive bikes, even though Russell won twice on his Kawasaki. Further confirmation came in the Italian race at Misano. Fogarty was still not entirely recovered, but his leadership in the Ducati team was taken over by Falappa, and a first-place and a second-place put the team back in the running for the world championship. Mauro Lucchiari, the prodigal son, also did some astonishing work. At the end of the previous season, Lucchiari had decided he would race for Yamaha, but the

relationship only lasted two races. At Misano he was back riding a Ducati, and on it he took a fifth- and a third-place.

At this point, all eyes were on Falappa. His confidence in his bike was perfect, and he was really riding to win. No Italian had yet won the Superbike world championship, and for Ducati it would be a memorable achievement were Falappa the one to win. All hopes of this were swept away, however, when Falappa had a very bad accident during a series of tests on the track at Albacete, Spain, the week before the Grand Prix race was to be run. Falappa was very badly injured, and for a number of days he hovered between life and death. Only on the eve of the race did the doctors give some indication that Falappa might well win his daunting race with death. It gave a new serenity and drive to the racers. Morale in Casa Ducati was further raised by a splendid double victory by Fogarty, accompanied by Whitham's two third-place finishes; the racers dedicated their victories to the hope that Falappa might yet race again. For Ducati, and especially for Fogarty, the championship was turning into a walk. In Austria, again, the finish seemed to be a carbon copy of what had happened in Spain. It was actually even better, since in both races the

85

OTHER DUCATI, RIDDEN by Meklau, FINISHED RIGHT BEHIND FOGARTY. THE REIGNING CHAMPION, RUSSELL, SEEMED TO BE PLUNGED INTO AN ABYSS OF DEEP DEPRESSION. NERVES IN TEAM DUCATI WERE TENSE: AT STAKE WAS THE VERY CREDIBILITY OF THE MOTORCYCLE. THE DUCATI TEAM SEEMED TO HAVE REGAINED A CERTAIN SERENITY by THE TIME THEY REACHED INDONESIA, SINCE IT WAS CLEAR THAT IF THEY WAS GOING TO WIN, IT WOULD NOT BE WITH FOGARTY ALONE, WHILE RUSSELL CONTINUED TO DO QUITE WELL. Actually, IN THE FIRST RACE, FOGARTY WAS FORCED TO RETIRE, LEAVING THE VICTORY TO his TEAMMATE WHITHAM. THE ENGLISH RACER REDEEMED HIMSELF by WINNING THE NEXT RACE, bUT THE DUCATI DID NOT SEEM TO bE HANDLING THIS TRIP TO THE FAR EAST VERY WELL. PIROVANO bROKE THE ENGINE TWICE, AND FEARS bEGAN TO SPREAD CONCERNING THE RELIABILITY OF THE bIKE. THAT FEAR VANISHED IN JAPAN. THIS TIME THE VALVE ROCKER ARMS, WHICH HAD CAUSED THE FORFEIT IN INDONESIA, WORKED PERFECTLY. THE WORK OF THE bOLOGNESE TECHNICIANS ELIMINATED ALL THE GLITCHES, THOUGH DUCATI STILL LOST TO RUSSELL'S KAWASAKI. FOGARTY PLACED SECOND AND FOURTH, bUT WAS READY TO REGAIN THE INITIATIVE IN HOLLAND TWO WEEKS LATER WHEN HE WON bOTH RACES AND LEFT RUSSELL WITH ONLY A PAIR OF SIXTH-PLACE FINISHES. THIS WAS A FINISH THAT ENCOURAGED HOPES FOR GOOD RESULTS IN THE NEXT RACE, THE SAN MARINO GRAND PRIX AT MUGELLO. IN THE FIRST RACE, HOWEVER, IT WAS RUSSELL WHO UPSET THE HOPES OF THE ITALIAN PUBLIC: HE WON, LEAVING bEHIND THE DUCATIS OF FOGARTY AND THE NEW AMERICAN SUPERBIKE CHAMPION, TROY CORSER. IN THIS SAME RACE, VIRGINIO FERRARI RETURNED TO THE TRACK, TAKING OFF his TEAM MANAGER HAT FOR ONCE, AND WEARING A RACER'S HELMET ONCE AGAIN. bUT THE TEAM COLORS WERE HELD HIGH ONCE AGAIN by FOGARTY, WHO WON THE SECOND RACE. RUSSELL WAS FORCED TO LEAVE THE RACE bECAUSE OF PROBLEMS WITH his KAWASAKI'S ENGINE WHILE DUCATI HAD FOUR bIKES IN THE FIRST FIVE PLACES AT THE FINISH, WITH LUCCHIARI THIRD, WHITHAM FOURTH, AND PIROVANO FIFTH.

TO OPEN THINGS UP AGAIN FOR THE WORLD CHAMPIONSHIP, ALL IT

TOOK WAS THE HOME TRACK RACE RUN by FOGARTY. THE EUROPEAN GRAND PRIX MOVED FROM JEREZ TO DONINGTON, FROM THE SUNSHINE OF SPAIN TO THE RAIN OF ENGLAND. bUT "FOGGY," AS FOGARTY IS CALLED by his FRIENDS, IS ANYTHING bUT A SPECIALIST IN RACING ON WET TARMAC, EVEN THOUGH THAT IS ONE OF THE MOST COMMON CONDITIONS ON ENGLISH RACE TRACKS. RUSSELL TOOK ADVANTAGE OF THE SITUATION AND WON bOTH RACES, WHILE his RIVAL TOOK ONLY A 14TH- AND A 5TH-PLACE FINISH. AND THAT FINISH THREW EVERYTHING INTO CHAOS AND CONFUSION ONCE AGAIN, ON THE EVE OF THE FINAL RACE. FOGARTY WAS LEADING THE CHAMPIONSHIP AT THIS POINT, bUT his LEAD WAS SLICED TO A SLIM FIVE POINTS. DUCATI CERTAINLY HAD A POWERFUL TEAM STANDING, WITH TWO SECOND-PLACES FROM CORSER AND A THIRD-PLACE FROM LUCCHIARI. THESE RESULTS WERE IMPORTANT ONES bECAUSE THEY ALLOWED DUCATI TO WIN THE WORLD MANUFACTURERS' TITLE ONE RACE EARLY.

THE MYSTERY OF WHO WOULD WIN WAS TO bE SOLVED IN AUSTRALIA. AT PHILLIPS ISLAND, FOGARTY AND RUSSELL RAN THE FINAL COMPETITION, NEVER FORGETTING THAT JUST bEHIND THEM WAS AARON SLIGHT. THE HONDA RACER HAD NEVER WON, bUT PLACING AS REGULARLY AS HE DID, HE WAS DOWN by ONLY 17 POINTS, AND THEREFORE HAD A CHANCE, HOWEVER REMOTE THAT CHANCE MAY HAVE bEEN. THAT CHANCE WAS bLOWN AWAY IN THE FIRST RACE by FOGARTY AND RUSSELL, WHO FINISHED IN THE FIRST TWO POSITIONS, WHILE SLIGHT WAS ONLY FOURTH. THE REMAINING RACE WOULD DETERMINE THE NAME OF THE WORLD CHAMPION OF 1994, JUST HALF AN HOUR TO DECIDE WHETHER DUCATI WOULD RETURN TO THE TOP AFTER THE TITLES WON by ROCHE AND POLEN, OR WHETHER KAWASAKI WOULD TAKE THE TITLE FOR THE SECOND YEAR RUNNING. THE CLEAR SUPERIORITY SHOWN by FOGARTY IN THE FIRST RACE, OR PERHAPS WE SHOULD SAY THE SUPERIORITY OF FOGARTY'S DUCATI OVER RUSSELL'S KAWASAKI, DASHED RUSSELL'S HOPES FOR GOOD. IF HE HAD TRULY WANTED TO bECOME CHAMPION AGAIN, HE WOULD HAVE SEIZED THE bIT AND RUN WITH IT, bUT WHEN HE REALIZED THAT THERE WAS NOTHING TO bE DONE, AND THAT his DUNLOP TIRES WERE SHARPLY

inferior to the Ducati's Michelins, Russell just threw in the towel. Fogarty could rest on his oars at this point: he was the new world champion, even if he slowed his pace and let the local hero Antony Gobert—a new member of the Kawasaki team and recent victor of the Australian championship—win the race.

This detailed analysis of the season was justified by the fact that during the 1994 world championship, Ducati won 12 races out of the 22 it ran, thus attaining its eighth world title in five years of racing in the Superbike championships: four racers' championships and as many manufacturers' championships. A cluster of honors that, on its own, confirms just how important the Desmoquattro series has been to the

history of motorcycle racing and how great has been the commitment of the Bologna-based manufacturer, with all its executives and technicians, to attain these remarkable results.

We should also give special recognition to the success attained by Troy Corser in the American Motorcyclist Association championship. Thanks to this victory, Ducati recorded its name in the honor rolls for the second time in a row; in the year previous, Doug Polen, riding the 888, had won this major title. But in the American races there is still one "black hole" for Casa Ducati: a win in the Daytona 200, perhaps the top of the entire international calendar. That is an objective that has so far been absent from the Ducati record book, at least through 1995.

916 Corsa 1994

Specifications

Engine: four-cycle, twin-cylinder "L" at 90 degrees. Liquid cooling, closed-circuit with curved radiator. Bore and stroke: 96x66 mm. Displacement: 955 cc. Compression ratio: 12:1 . Maximum power: 150 hp/EEC/shaft at 11,500 rpm . Timing: dual overhead cam shaft, four valves per cylinder driven by a toothed belt with aluminum pulleys, desmodromic system. Valve diameters: 37 mm intake, 31 mm exhaust. Timing diagram: intake open 31 degrees BTDC, close 78 degrees ABDC; exhaust open 71 degrees BBDC, close 45 degrees ATDC. Lubrication: forced, with geared pump and cooling radiator on the circuit. Circuit capacity: 4 kg. Fuel injection: Weber indirect electronic injection Alfa/N with two injectors per cylinder. Ignition: electronic I.A.W. type with inductive discharge, small generator, light, single-piece flywheel with support flange. Transmission: primary with straight-tooth gearing, secondary by chain. Gears: six speeds. Clutch: multi-disk dry type with hydraulic control. Frame: open latticework with engine as a stressed element of the structure, round tubes made from 25 Cr Mo 4 steel. Suspension: front, Öhlins upside-down fork, adjustable for rebound, damping, and preload; 46 mm shafts with 120 mm stroke, adjustable for rebound; rear, single-sided swing arm with Öhlins progressive single shock-absorber, adjustable for rebound, damping, and preload; wheel travel, 120 mm Wheels: rims in magnesium alloy, with five spokes, front 3.50x17, rear, in magnesium alloy, with three spokes, 6.0x17. Tires, front 12/60x17 SC 1275 Michelin, rear 18/76 - 17 SC 1876 Michelin. Brakes: front, 320-mm floating double disk, in carbon, with calipers with four-piston calipers; rear, 200-mm disk. Wheelbase: 1,420 mm. Max. length: 2,050 mm. Height of seat: 790 mm. Trail: 91–97 mm. Inclination of the steering column: 24 degrees 30 minutes. Fuel tank capacity: 22 liters. Dry weight: 150 kg. Note: The fuel tank, fairing, seat, and air intake housing are all made of a carbon-fiber/Kevlar composite material.

916 SENNA

On the eve of the Motor Show 1994, a certain air of mystery surrounded the new bikes and features that Ducati was expected to introduce that year. That air of mystery was heightened considerably by the platform that was left empty inside the Ducati stand. That mystery was not dispelled until the fair was already well under way, when the empty platform was occupied by the 916 Senna, a motorcycle that had been developed in close cooperation with the much-lamented late Formula 1 champion driver.

The motorcycle may have been presented with some slight delay, but the manner of its presentation more than made up for its timing; among those present were Vivian Senna Lalli, the sister of the late racer, and Carl Fogarty, the motorcycle racer who, more than any other, had been responsible for the fame of the 916. For this new and more exclusive version of the Desmoquattro, the name Senna was not merely a "designer name," or a prestige endorsement intended to enhance the motorcycle's image. Not that the late Ayrton Senna would have agreed to allow his name to be used in such a manner; and not that Ducati had the slightest need to promote the image of their best known and most respected model, in any case. The reason for the collaboration arose from Ayrton's great interest in motorcycle racing, and from his close ties of friendship with the brothers Gianfranco and Claudio Castiglioni, heads of the Cagiva Group, in turn owner of

Ducati Motorcycles. In order to have some understanding of the role that Ayrton Senna played, simply consider a few samples of what he described as his own guiding philosophy of life: "To have raced and to have succeeded in remaining Number One in Formula One for many years now has greatly influenced my character: it has pushed me to strive tirelessly to be better, to be completely professional, and to reach for perfection. If you want to be successful, you have to give your all, and sometimes even more." Senna was always true to this credo, both in racing and in his private life.

It was no accident that on March 7, 1994, less than two months before the terrible crash at Imola which took his life, Senna had approved all of the modifications that were to go into the Ducati that would bear his name. His enormous body of knowledge in racing was thus transferred to a model of motorcycle that was meant for the mass public, although the conditions of use were still taken carefully into account. The basic foundation was the street version of the 916. Senna then prescribed a series of modifications that were capable of merging the bike's competitive nature with certain exclusive technical and aesthetic solutions. In the context of the tradition of the various Desmoquattro motorcycles, the color pattern veered sharply away from the traditional red in favor of a two-tone pattern of black and grey. The visual contrast was heightened by the hubs, which were painted red.

The power plant remained the same, capable of delivering a

On these two pages, the 916 Senna and a portrait of the late champion Formula 1 racer. The modifications made to the 916, made in a series limited to only 300, were recommended and tested by Senna himself. On the previous double-page, Fogarty (2) shooting toward world victory and the American racer, Troy Corser, left, at the winners' stand in the AMA Superbike championship, in 1994. In the other picture, note Virginio Ferrari at the Italian Grand Prix. For once, he has doffed the hat of team manager, and donned a racer's helmet.

maximum power output well over 100 hp, as did the frame. The components, on the other hand, were quite a different matter, as Senna's enormous racing experience made it possible to transfer a number of details from the Racing version onto this model, without however undercutting its destination as a street model. The fairing, the mudguards, and the chain casing were all made of carbon fiber, as were the two mufflers and the clutch casing.

Also meant to combine lightness with strength, the little framework supporting the seat was made of aluminum, while in order to make the bike easier to drive, the front-brake lever and the clutch lever were adjustable. Compared with the "basic" version of 1995, the differences in the Senna version had to do with the single rider seat; the front brake mechanism, featuring a double floating disk in cast iron; braided stainless steel brake lines; and the rear shock-absorber, by Öhlins instead of Showa. These were

modifications that helped to improve performance and safety, though they in no way interfered with the street-worthiness of the bike. The 916 Senna stood at the peak of the array of Ducati street bikes, because of its exclusiveness (it was produced in a limited series of just 300 bikes). This latter decision was in accord with the Senna Foundation, an organization set up in 1990 by the Brazilian racer—and headed since his death by his sister Vivian—to oversee the distribution of all those products that bear his name. Like everything else that bears the Senna trademark, all the profits from the 916 Senna are given to charity, especially programs for the welfare and development of the children of Brazil and the rest of the world. The 916 Senna stands as a demonstration of the late Ayrton Senna's real interest in the world of motorcycles, an interest that had driven him to undertake a collaborative relationship with Ducati and with the brothers Castiglioni.

916 Senna

Specifications

Engine: four-cycle, twin-cylinder "L" at 90 degrees. Liquid cooling, closed-circuit with curved radiator with thermostat. Bore and stroke: 94x66 mm Displacement: 916 cc. Compression ratio: 11:1 . Maximum power: 109 hp/EEC/shaft at 9,000 rpm . Timing: dual overhead cam shaft, four valves per cylinder driven by a toothed belt, desmodromic system. Valve diameters: 33 mm intake, 29 mm exhaust. Timing diagram: intake open 11 degrees ATDC, close 70 degrees ABDC; exhaust open 60 degrees ABDC, close 18 degrees ATDC. Lubrication: forced, with geared pump and cooling radiator on the circuit. Circuit capacity: 4 kg. Fuel injection: Weber indirect electronic injection Alfa/N CPU 1.6 M with one injector per cylinder. Ignition: electronic I.A.W. type with inductive discharge. Transmission: primary with straight-tooth gearing, secondary by chain. Gears: six speeds. Clutch: multi-disk dry type with hydraulic control. Frame: tubular, with lattice-work, overhead cage made of ALS 450 steel tubes. Suspension: front, Showa upside-down fork, adjustable for rebound and damping, as well as preload, 43 mm shafts with 120 mm stroke; rear, oscillating single-sided swingarm with Öhlins single shock-absorber, adjustable for rebound, damping, and preload, wheel travel, 130 mm. Wheels: rims in light alloy, front 3.50x17, rear 5.50x17. Tires, front 120/60x17, rear 190/50x17. Brakes: front, 320-mm floating double disk, with calipers with four differentiated pistons; rear, 220-mm disk. Wheelbase: 1,410 mm. Max. length: 2,050 mm Height of seat: 790 mm. Steering angle: 27 degrees. Trail: 91–97 mm. Inclination of the steering column, in two positions: 23 degrees 30 minutes or 24 degrees 30 minutes. Fuel tank capacity: 17 liters. Dry weight: 201 kg., ready to ride, without fuel.

THE "LITTLE" DESMOQUATTRO

In 1995, the range of displacements of Ducati twin-cylinder "L" engines was extended to include the 748 cc.

At first glance, the 748 could be easily confused with the 916; the general appearance was similar, as were the components and the technical layout. And yet, the 748 Biposto—as the street version of the "smallest" twin-cylinder motorcycle of the Desmoquattro series is called—can certainly boast a personality all its own. And, if at first, one might mistake it for a "baby sister" of the 916, all one need do is examine it carefully and in detail and ride it, and it will become clear that the 748 shines with its own—and not merely reflected—light. The reflected light, however brilliant,

of the 916 and its racing victories, do nothing to enhance the 748's luster: its identity is so well established that none of this is necessary to capture the attention of aficionados.

All the same, it is not easy to tell the 748 from the 916. Only the different decals on the fairing, along with the wheels and a metal grill that protects the air intake at the bottom of the fairing, distinguish it. Everything else, from color of the body to the components, is quite similar. Both the 748 and the 916 make use of 17-inch wheels, but for the 748, the tires are 120/60 and 180/55, while on the 916 the tires are 120/70 and 190/50. The 748 engine—though it may be smaller than the 916 and all the other previous

DESMOQUATTROS, SUCH AS THE 851 AND THE 888—HAS THE SAME TECHNICAL FEATURES. Of COURSE, THE MOST distinctive features could hardly be changed: the 90-degree, "L" twin-cylinder arrangement and the electronic fuel injection. As on all street models with larger engines, beginning with the second version of the 851, the Weber injection system consists of a single injector per cylinder. The 6-speed transmission, although the ratios of the last four gears were changed, is substantially the same as that of the 916, as is the dry clutch. And the same is true of the valve mechanism, which features dual overhead cam shafts and four valves per cylinder driven by a toothed belt. Even the ignition curve was the same as that of the 916, just as the diameter and the lift of the intake and exhaust valves remain the same as in the larger engine. The only real differences between the power plant of the 748 and that of the 916 are the fundamental measurements: 88x61.5 bore and stroke instead of 94x66 and maximum power of 98 hp for the 748 versus the 916's 109 hp. That translates into a top speed of roughly 15 km/h less for the "little sister," 245 km/h instead of 260 km/h. In the wheel mechanism and in the frame, apart from the different size of the tires, nothing is different. As on the 916, the lattice-style, steel-tube frame has the possibility of adjusting the inclination of the steering shaft to an angle of 23 degrees 30 minutes or else to 24 degrees 30 minutes. This variation affects the rake, too, shifting it from 91 mm to 97 mm, though it has no effect on the wheelbase length. There are no changes in the suspension or the braking system from the 916. The front tire is carried by a Showa upside-down fork, with 43 mm fork legs and 120 mm of travel.

Like the single rear shock absorber, the front forks are adjustable for rebound, damping, and preload. At the rear, the shock absorber is attached to the handsome single-sided swing arm, cast in a light alloy, with the wheel, attached by overhang. The brakes consist of 320-mm floating double discs in the front clamped by four-piston calipers and a 220-mm disc in the rear. The close kinship of the 748 to the 916, also resulted in the smaller model having the same modifications that had been applied in 1995 to the "flagship" of the series as opposed to the features found on the previous year's 916.

On both motorcycles the connecting rods were moulded, the computer that controls injection was the new 1.6M type, the frame was reinforced, the chain cover was longer, and the electrical system had hermetically sealed relays. A technical analysis of the 748 might make the reader think of it as a small-scale copy of the 916, even though this motorcycle has the same engine displacement as the very first Ducati Desmoquattro built back in 1986. If, however, we take a practical look at how the 748 and 916 perform under actual road conditions, we will discover that, even though the bikes are similar in terms of performance (although the 748 does not have the same "response" as the 916 at low and medium rpms), they handle in completely different ways.

The 748 is even easier and more intuitive than the 916. When you enter a curve, the 748 sets up a more immediate and precise trajectory, even if the front end tends to lighten up somewhat more. This adds up to greater speed in entering and negotiating curves than is offered even by the 916. This, it is safe to say, makes the 748 not only the "queen" of its category (comparable with four-cylinder 600 cc bikes), but puts it in a first-place position in absolute terms. That applies to expense, as well, since the 1995 price of 22,839,000 Italian lire puts it beyond the reach of many a would-be owners.

The 748, both in the Biposto and in the SP versions, aesthetically harkens back to the lines we found on the 916. Only the 748 SP stands out for its unprecedented bright yellow. In technical terms, the 748 is nothing more than a smaller copy of the 916, although we should keep in mind that its displacement is the same as the displacement with which Ducati debuted the four-valve desmodromic engine, forerunner to this one. In comparison with the 916, the main difference lies in the performance, since the 748 has 98 hp, while the 916 has 109

A "MINIATURE" BEAST, THE 748 S.P.

An S.P. version of 748 was also produced for 1995. In comparison with the Biposto of the same displacement, the S.P. differs by its yellow color and its tail, with white number space. Among the technical details, we should mention the single rear shock absorber, made by Öhlins instead of Showa; the front disc brakes, made of cast iron instead of steel; the front brake lines of braided stainless steel; the oil cooler; and the adjustable front brake lever The engine has a slightly greater compression ratio and a different timing curve, the two yielding an increase of 6 hp. The S.P. weighs 2 kg less than the Biposto version even though the S.P. has no carbon-fiber components, as is the case with the counterpart version of the 916. And, again in comparison with the 916, the difference in price between the two versions is less marked. In 1995, the S.P. cost 26,650,000 Italian lire, as against 22,700,000 for the Biposto.

Ducati 748 Biposto (748 S.P.) 1995
Specifications

Engine: four-cycle, twin-cylinder "L" at 90 degrees, with aluminum cylinders with silicon carbide facing. Liquid cooling, closed-circuit with curved radiator with thermostat. Bore and stroke: 88x61.5 mm Displacement: 748 cc. Compression ratio: 11.5:1 (11.6:1). Maximum power: 98 hp/EEC/shaft at 11,000 rpm (104 hp/EEC/shaft). Timing: dual overhead cam shaft, four valves per cylinder driven by a toothed belt, desmodromic system. Valve diameters: 33 mm intake, 29 mm exhaust. Timing diagram: intake opens 11 degrees BTDC, close 70 degrees ABDC (44 degrees ATDC, 72 degrees ABDC); exhaust open 62 degrees BBDC, close 18 degrees ATDC. (77 degrees ABDC, 42 degrees ATDC). Lubrication: forced, with geared pump (radiator on the circuit). Capacity of the lubrication circuit: 3.5 kg. (4 kg.). Fuel injection: Weber indirect electronic injection Alfa/N CPU 1.6 M with one injector per cylinder. Ignition: electronic I.A.W. type with inductive discharge. Transmission: primary with straight-tooth gearing, secondary by chain. Gears: six speeds. Clutch: multi-disk dry type with hydraulic control. Frame: tubular, with lattice-work, overhead cage made of ALS 450 steel tubes. Suspension: front, Showa upside-down fork, adjustable for rebound, damping, and preload, 43 mm shafts with 120 mm stroke; rear, oscillating single-sided swingarm with Showa (Öhlins) single shock-absorber, adjustable for rebound, damping, and preload, shock-absorber stroke 71 mm, wheel range, 130 mm. Wheels: 3-spoke rims in light alloy, front 3.50x17, rear 5.50x17, with flexible coupling. Tires, front 120/60x17, rear 180/55x17. Brakes: front, 320-mm double disk (cast-iron 320-mm double disk), with calipers with four pistons; rear, 220-mm disk. Wheelbase: 1,410 mm Max. length: 2,050 mm Height of seat: 790 mm Steering angle: 27 degrees. Rake: 91–97 mm. Inclination of the steering column, in two positions: 29 degrees 30 minutes or 24 degrees 30 minutes. Fuel tank capacity: 17 liters. Dry weight: 202 kg. (200 kg.).

THE FUTURE OF THE DESMOQUATTRO

The technical superiority of the 916, so clearly demonstrated during the 1994 world championships, was plain to see once again in 1995. Indeed, the first races of the season showed a virtually absolute dominance by the racers riding Ducati motorcycles. In fact, while waiting to see if they have won yet another world title, Ducati has the consolation of boasting its hundredth—that's right, 100th!—victory in a world championship race, going back only to 1988. And this performance was not the result of a new motorcycle, but with the same 916 that so dominated the races last year.

Between the 1994 version Corsa and the 1995, there are truly only minimal differences: improved camshafts designed to limit strain on the valves, different valve material, and finally, exhaust pipes enlarged in diameter from 50 to 52 mm. The modifications in the wheel mechanisms were minimal, too, concerning the swing arm and the hub of the rear wheel—both made of magnesium. The front discs were different as well, made of steel now instead of carbon: not because of any ideas of the Ducati technicians or racers, but to comply with the new regulations established by the international federation. These regulations attempted to question Ducati's supremacy by raising the minimum weight allowed for motorcycles with twin-cylinder engines. Even though this

reduced the difference—at least on the scales—from the four-cylinder motorcycles, it did nothing to narrow the technical gap that allowed Ducatis to dominate the world championship. Even if the motorcycles were clearly superior, Ducati continued its search for higher quality. Just the history of the Desmoquattro series is quite sufficient to show that the Ducati technicians have not been resting on their laurels. And not only in the field of track competition. Unlike earlier days, however, the on-track triumphs were matched by equal success in the marketplace. Monthly output of Ducatis hovers around 1,500 motorcycles, with the bikes of the Desmoquattro series representing about 40 percent. This is too large a share to be overlooked, in part because of the spectacular image effect, but also because of its role as a locomotive for the other models. In the Ducati technical offices, then, the focus is on the future, with a keen attention on the Desmoquattro of the 21st century. The assistants of Engineer Bordi are working on what they call the next development of the current (1995) version, even though all that remains in this engine are the original concepts that defined the Desmoquattro series.

Between the present and the future, the only common bonds are, or will be, the twin-cylinder scheme with a 90-degree "L" layout, desmodromic timing, four valves per cylinder, liquid cooling, and electronic fuel injection. The four pillars of Ducati engineering.

These are the only elements of continuity. No detail is interchangeable. If what we might call the first phase of the Desmoquattro series saw the motorcycle developing around the engine, in the next series the engine will have to work to keep pace with the motorcycle, especially the frame. The engineers will seek a solution that makes it possible to contain the overall size while reducing the wheelbase and improving weight distribution.

A general overhaul will have its effect on the engine displacement, since lightness and the perfect aerodynamic penetration make it possible to obtain superb performance with even a "small" engine, such as a 750 cc. These are all projects that are still on paper, because of the enormous racing and commercial success of the 916 and 748, but ready to materialize as soon as the situation changes, in order to maintain the quality and superiority that has made the Desmoquattro a great masterpiece of Italian motorcycle technology.